Proper Education Group

4 Practice Tests for the Georgia Real Estate Exam

—

"The secret to getting ahead is getting started."
Mark Twain

Table of Contents

Introduction

1.1 Requirements

On the day of the test, you must bring the following:

1. **TWO** forms of valid and non-expired government-issued ID with a valid signature. One must be government issued and include a photo. Examples include:
   a. Driver's license
   b. State issued identification (ex. non-driver ID)
   c. United States Passport
   d. Credit card
2. A second ID that contains your signature and legal name
3. A basic non-scientific calculator

You are not required to bring a calculator, but you are **highly encouraged to do so** as there will be simple mathematical questions that require multiplication and division. Do not rely on the one on your phone because **phones will not be allowed**.

1.2 About the Exam

The test is 4 hours long and composed of two sections.

The national portion is composed of 100 multiple choice questions.

The state portion is composed of 52 multiple choice questions.

The passing score for the exam is calculated using an abstract formula called the Angoff method. From the official Candidate Handbook: "The minimum score required to pass the multiple-choice portions is determined by using a process known as the Angoff method, in which subject-matter experts estimate the difficulty of each item on the examination for the "minimally competent practitioner" (MCP). These judgments are averaged to determine the minimum passing score, which represents the amount of knowledge an MCP would likely demonstrate on the examination."

The exam is administered through a computer.

1.3 How to Apply

To apply for the exam, visit the website below and submit the required the forms:

http://documents.goamp.com/Publications/candidateHandbooks/GAREP-handbook.pdf

All of the official documentation pertaining payments, documents, and forms can be found there.

1.4 Exam Results

Your score will be given to you immediately after finishing the exam.

Practice Test 1

Directions:

1. You have a 4-hour time limit to complete the whole exam.

2. To pass, aim to answer at least 75 out of 100 questions correctly on the national portion **AND** at least 39 out of 52 questions on the state portion.

3. Some questions will require mathematics. You may use a calculator.

4. **Phones and pagers are not allowed. Having either will result in automatic dismissal from the exam and nullification of exam scores.**

Tips:

- Answer all questions even if you are unsure.
- Mark any questions you are stuck on and revisit them after you are done. The exam is timed so make sure you finish as many questions as you can.
- After reading the question, try answering it in your head first to avoid getting confused by the choices.
- Read the entire question before looking at the answers.
- Use the process of elimination to filter out choices that don't seem correct to increase your chances of selecting the correct answer.
- Be aware of important keywords like **not, sometimes, always,** and **never**. These words completely alter the ask of the question so it's important to keep track of them.

PLEASE READ THESE INSTRUCTIONS CAREFULLY.

Practice Test 1

Name: Belinda   Date: 8/27

NATIONAL PORTION

	A B C D		A B C D		A B C D		A B C D
1.	Ⓐ Ⓑ Ⓒ Ⓓ	31.	Ⓐ Ⓑ Ⓒ Ⓓ	61.	Ⓐ Ⓑ Ⓒ Ⓓ	91.	Ⓐ Ⓑ Ⓒ Ⓓ
2.	Ⓐ Ⓑ Ⓒ Ⓓ	32.	Ⓐ Ⓑ Ⓒ Ⓓ	62.	Ⓐ Ⓑ Ⓒ Ⓓ	92.	Ⓐ Ⓑ Ⓒ Ⓓ
3.	Ⓐ Ⓑ Ⓒ Ⓓ	33.	Ⓐ Ⓑ Ⓒ Ⓓ	63.	Ⓐ Ⓑ Ⓒ Ⓓ	93.	Ⓐ Ⓑ Ⓒ Ⓓ
4.	Ⓐ Ⓑ Ⓒ Ⓓ	34.	Ⓐ Ⓑ Ⓒ Ⓓ	64.	Ⓐ Ⓑ Ⓒ Ⓓ	94.	Ⓐ Ⓑ Ⓒ Ⓓ
5.	Ⓐ Ⓑ Ⓒ Ⓓ	35.	Ⓐ Ⓑ Ⓒ Ⓓ	65.	Ⓐ Ⓑ Ⓒ Ⓓ	95.	Ⓐ Ⓑ Ⓒ Ⓓ
6.	Ⓐ Ⓑ Ⓒ Ⓓ	36.	Ⓐ Ⓑ Ⓒ Ⓓ	66.	Ⓐ Ⓑ Ⓒ Ⓓ	96.	Ⓐ Ⓑ Ⓒ Ⓓ
7.	Ⓐ Ⓑ Ⓒ Ⓓ	37.	Ⓐ Ⓑ Ⓒ Ⓓ	67.	Ⓐ Ⓑ Ⓒ Ⓓ	97.	Ⓐ Ⓑ Ⓒ Ⓓ
8.	Ⓐ Ⓑ Ⓒ Ⓓ	38.	Ⓐ Ⓑ Ⓒ Ⓓ	68.	Ⓐ Ⓑ Ⓒ Ⓓ	98.	Ⓐ Ⓑ Ⓒ Ⓓ
9.	Ⓐ Ⓑ Ⓒ Ⓓ	39.	Ⓐ Ⓑ Ⓒ Ⓓ	69.	Ⓐ Ⓑ Ⓒ Ⓓ	99.	Ⓐ Ⓑ Ⓒ Ⓓ
10.	Ⓐ Ⓑ Ⓒ Ⓓ	40.	Ⓐ Ⓑ Ⓒ Ⓓ	70.	Ⓐ Ⓑ Ⓒ Ⓓ	100.	Ⓐ Ⓑ Ⓒ Ⓓ
11.	Ⓐ Ⓑ Ⓒ Ⓓ	41.	Ⓐ Ⓑ Ⓒ Ⓓ	71.	Ⓐ Ⓑ Ⓒ Ⓓ		
12.	Ⓐ Ⓑ Ⓒ Ⓓ	42.	Ⓐ Ⓑ Ⓒ Ⓓ	72.	Ⓐ Ⓑ Ⓒ Ⓓ		
13.	Ⓐ Ⓑ Ⓒ Ⓓ	43.	Ⓐ Ⓑ Ⓒ Ⓓ	73.	Ⓐ Ⓑ Ⓒ Ⓓ		
14.	Ⓐ Ⓑ Ⓒ Ⓓ	44.	Ⓐ Ⓑ Ⓒ Ⓓ	74.	Ⓐ Ⓑ Ⓒ Ⓓ		
15.	Ⓐ Ⓑ Ⓒ Ⓓ	45.	Ⓐ Ⓑ Ⓒ Ⓓ	75.	Ⓐ Ⓑ Ⓒ Ⓓ		
16.	Ⓐ Ⓑ Ⓒ Ⓓ	46.	Ⓐ Ⓑ Ⓒ Ⓓ	76.	Ⓐ Ⓑ Ⓒ Ⓓ		
17.	Ⓐ Ⓑ Ⓒ Ⓓ	47.	Ⓐ Ⓑ Ⓒ Ⓓ	77.	Ⓐ Ⓑ Ⓒ Ⓓ		
18.	Ⓐ Ⓑ Ⓒ Ⓓ	48.	Ⓐ Ⓑ Ⓒ Ⓓ	78.	Ⓐ Ⓑ Ⓒ Ⓓ		
19.	Ⓐ Ⓑ Ⓒ Ⓓ	49.	Ⓐ Ⓑ Ⓒ Ⓓ	79.	Ⓐ Ⓑ Ⓒ Ⓓ		
20.	Ⓐ Ⓑ Ⓒ Ⓓ	50.	Ⓐ Ⓑ Ⓒ Ⓓ	80.	Ⓐ Ⓑ Ⓒ Ⓓ		
21.	Ⓐ Ⓑ Ⓒ Ⓓ	51.	Ⓐ Ⓑ Ⓒ Ⓓ	81.	Ⓐ Ⓑ Ⓒ Ⓓ		
22.	Ⓐ Ⓑ Ⓒ Ⓓ	52.	Ⓐ Ⓑ Ⓒ Ⓓ	82.	Ⓐ Ⓑ Ⓒ Ⓓ		
23.	Ⓐ Ⓑ Ⓒ Ⓓ	53.	Ⓐ Ⓑ Ⓒ Ⓓ	83.	Ⓐ Ⓑ Ⓒ Ⓓ		
24.	Ⓐ Ⓑ Ⓒ Ⓓ	54.	Ⓐ Ⓑ Ⓒ Ⓓ	84.	Ⓐ Ⓑ Ⓒ Ⓓ		
25.	Ⓐ Ⓑ Ⓒ Ⓓ	55.	Ⓐ Ⓑ Ⓒ Ⓓ	85.	Ⓐ Ⓑ Ⓒ Ⓓ		
26.	Ⓐ Ⓑ Ⓒ Ⓓ	56.	Ⓐ Ⓑ Ⓒ Ⓓ	86.	Ⓐ Ⓑ Ⓒ Ⓓ		
27.	Ⓐ Ⓑ Ⓒ Ⓓ	57.	Ⓐ Ⓑ Ⓒ Ⓓ	87.	Ⓐ Ⓑ Ⓒ Ⓓ		
28.	Ⓐ Ⓑ Ⓒ Ⓓ	58.	Ⓐ Ⓑ Ⓒ Ⓓ	88.	Ⓐ Ⓑ Ⓒ Ⓓ		
29.	Ⓐ Ⓑ Ⓒ Ⓓ	59.	Ⓐ Ⓑ Ⓒ Ⓓ	89.	Ⓐ Ⓑ Ⓒ Ⓓ		
30.	Ⓐ Ⓑ Ⓒ Ⓓ	60.	Ⓐ Ⓑ Ⓒ Ⓓ	90.	Ⓐ Ⓑ Ⓒ Ⓓ		

Practice Test 1

Name: Belinda   Date: 8/27

STATE PORTION

#	A	B	C	D		#	A	B	C	D
1.	Ⓐ	Ⓑ	Ⓒ	●		31. Ⓑ	●	Ⓑ	Ⓒ	Ⓓ
2.	●	Ⓑ	Ⓒ	Ⓓ		32.	Ⓐ	Ⓑ	●	Ⓓ
3.	Ⓐ	●	Ⓒ	Ⓓ		33.	Ⓐ	Ⓑ	Ⓒ	●
4.	●	Ⓑ	Ⓒ	Ⓓ		34.	Ⓐ	Ⓑ	●	Ⓓ
5. B	●	Ⓑ	Ⓒ	Ⓓ		35.	Ⓐ	Ⓑ	Ⓒ	●
6.	Ⓐ	Ⓑ	●	Ⓓ		36.	Ⓐ	Ⓑ	Ⓒ	●
7. B	●	Ⓑ	Ⓒ	Ⓓ		37.	Ⓐ	●	Ⓒ	Ⓓ
8.	Ⓐ	Ⓑ	●	Ⓓ		38.	Ⓐ	Ⓑ	●	Ⓓ
9.	Ⓐ	●	Ⓒ	Ⓓ		39. B	Ⓐ	Ⓑ	Ⓒ	●
10.	Ⓐ	Ⓑ	Ⓒ	●		40.	●	Ⓑ	Ⓒ	Ⓓ
11.	Ⓐ	Ⓑ	Ⓒ	●		41.	●	Ⓑ	Ⓒ	Ⓓ
12.	●	Ⓑ	Ⓒ	Ⓓ		42.	●	Ⓑ	Ⓒ	Ⓓ
13.	Ⓐ	Ⓑ	Ⓒ	●		43. A	Ⓐ	●	Ⓒ	Ⓓ
14.	●	Ⓑ	Ⓒ	Ⓓ		44.	Ⓐ	Ⓑ	Ⓒ	●
15.	Ⓐ	●	Ⓒ	Ⓓ		45. C	●	Ⓑ	Ⓒ	Ⓓ
16. A	Ⓐ	Ⓑ	Ⓒ	●		46.	Ⓐ	●	Ⓒ	Ⓓ
17.	Ⓐ	Ⓑ	●	Ⓓ		47.	Ⓐ	●	Ⓒ	Ⓓ
18.	Ⓐ	●	Ⓒ	Ⓓ		48.	Ⓐ	●	Ⓒ	Ⓓ
19.	●	Ⓑ	Ⓒ	Ⓓ		49.	Ⓐ	Ⓑ	●	Ⓓ
20. C	Ⓐ	Ⓑ	Ⓒ	●		50.	Ⓐ	Ⓑ	Ⓒ	●
21.	Ⓐ	●	Ⓒ	Ⓓ		51. C	●	Ⓑ	Ⓒ	Ⓓ
22.	●	Ⓑ	Ⓒ	Ⓓ		52.	Ⓐ	Ⓑ	Ⓒ	●
23.	Ⓐ	Ⓑ	Ⓒ	●						
24.	●	Ⓑ	Ⓒ	Ⓓ						
25. C	Ⓐ	✗	Ⓒ	●						
26. B	Ⓐ	Ⓑ	●	✗						
27.	●	Ⓑ	✗	Ⓓ						
28. B	Ⓐ	Ⓑ	●	Ⓓ						
29.	Ⓐ	Ⓑ	●	Ⓓ						
30.	Ⓐ	●	Ⓒ	Ⓓ						

National Portion

1. When applying for a loan, what is a **fixed rate**?

    A. A loan that has a predetermined repayment interest rate
    B. A loan that has an interest rate that varies over time
    C. A loan that accrues no interest
    D. A loan that pays off the interest before the principal

2. What act prohibits discrimination based on race or color?

    A. Fair Housing Act
    B. Civil Rights Act of 1866
    C. Civil Right Act of 1964
    D. Civil Rights Act Amendment of 1974

3. What is the financial document that contains a written promise to fulfill a certain payment?

    A. Invoice
    B. Promissory note
    C. Pro forma statement
    D. IOU

4. What is the term used to describe the act of replacing an existing mortgage with another?

    A. Refinancing
    B. Defaulting
    C. Foreclosure
    D. Reinvesting

5. Which is **not** an appurtenant right?

    A. Furnace
    B. Swimming pool
    C. Air conditioning
    D. All of the above

6. What is the name given to the banking option that allows a customer to deposit a specified amount for a predetermined period of time?

    A. Certificate of occupation
    B. Certificate of deposit
    C. Investment clause
    D. Mortgage

7. If a seller nets $225,000 after paying a 10% fee, what was the total he received?

    A. $202,500
    B. $224,990
    C. $250,000
    D. None of the above

8. What is the name given to the rate earned for borrowing or an investment per year?

    A. Rate lock
    B. Fixed rate
    C. Floating rate
    D. Annual percentage rate

9. Other than buying a home using traditional channels, what other methods can a prospective owner use to buy a home?

   A. Public auctions
   B. Tender
   C. Lease
   D. Escalation clause

10. What is the reviewing of a borrower's credit worthiness prior to loan approval?

   A. Buydown
   B. Pre-qualification
   C. Credit score
   D. Under qualification

11. What is the document that is used to transfer legal rights to act in the interest of a person?

   A. Disclosure form
   B. Power of attorney
   C. Pro forma statement
   D. Deed

12. What type of listing only guarantees commission for a sale within a specified period?

   A. Exclusive listing
   B. Net listing
   C. Single agency listing
   D. Multi agency listing

13. What type of brokerage mandates that the broker acts in the best interest of the buyer?

   A. Single agency
   B. Dual agency
   C. Multi agency
   D. Full service

14. What is the name of a transaction where both the buyer and seller are seeking the best deal?

   A. Real estate transaction
   B. Credit transaction
   C. Arms-length transaction
   D. Debited transaction

15. What is the name given to modification of billing calculation dates?

   A. Modified date
   B. Closing date
   C. Opening date
   D. Adjustment date

16. What is the name of the mortgage that is transferred by the seller to the buyer?

   A. Assumable mortgage
   B. Adjusted rate mortgage
   C. Fixed rate mortgage
   D. Floating mortgage

17. What is the contract that secures a future transaction?

    A. Deed
    B. Call option
    C. Title
    D. None of the above

18. What does an exclusive listing contract need to be considered valid?

    A. A net listing
    B. A commission rate of at least 6%
    C. A specified expiration date
    D. The signature of the grantee

19. What is it when another state recognizes your real estate license?

    A. Transfer
    B. Limited basis policy
    C. Reciprocity
    D. None of the above

20. Which of the following is **not** a fiduciary duty?

    A. Accounting
    B. Confidentiality
    C. Obedience
    D. Privacy

21. What are contingencies as used in real estate?

    A. Conditions that must be met by both the buyer and the seller before closing
    B. Conditions set by the government on buying a home
    C. Conditions set by the bank in order to approve a loan for a mortgage
    D. Conditions that must be met to avoid judicial foreclosure

22. Who is a co-borrower?

    A. Any individual whose name appears on the loan document
    B. Someone that borrows money at the same time with you
    C. The mortgage broker that originates the loan for you
    D. An individual that guarantees your loan

23. What is the name given to a loan taken out to finance construction?

    A. Mortgage
    B. Construction loan
    C. Business loan
    D. Personal loan

24. What is the name given to the inspection done by the buyer before closing?

    A. Final inspection
    B. Advertorial
    C. Housing ratio
    D. Final walkthrough

25. What is the name given to a mortgage whose interest rate does **not** change throughout the payment period?

    A. Adjustable mortgage rate
    B. Floating rate
    C. Fixed mortgage rate
    D. Bridge loan

26. What is defined as the percentage owned by the buyer after making a down payment?

    A. Housing ratio
    B. Debt to income ratio
    C. Loan to value ratio
    D. Floating rate

27. What is the cash on cash return of a $60,000 investment that generates $1,000 in monthly cash flow?

    Annual cash flow / Total investment

    A. 1.67%
    B. 2%
    C. 20%
    D. None of the above

28. What is the term used to refer to the responsibility one individual has for the acts of another?

    A. Vicarious liability
    B. Fixed liability
    C. Current liability
    D. Contingent

29. What is the name given to a form used to explain the role of an agent in a real estate transaction?

    A. Purchase agreement
    B. Accountability
    C. Assignment contract
    D. Agency disclosure statement

30. A number of brokers agreed on a set standard commission. What antitrust law are they guilty of violating?

    A. Commingling
    B. Price fixing
    C. Steering
    D. Discussing

31. Which government agency is responsible for determining the status of an independent contractor?

    A. Federal government
    B. Bank
    C. Department of State
    D. IRS

32. What is the nature of the title issued in condo ownership?

    A. Freehold
    B. Regular
    C. Deed
    D. Clear title

33. Mr. and Mrs. Johnson made a $350,000 profit on the sale of their primary home. How much do they owe in capital gains tax?

    A. $0
    B. $3,500
    C. $50,000
    D. Half of the amount earned

34. What is the status of an agent's license once it is revoked?

    A. Pending
    B. Cancelled
    C. Breached
    D. Suspended

35. Which insurance policy provides extra liability coverage for the insured party?

    A. Umbrella policy
    B. Home insurance
    C. Flood insurance
    D. Hazard insurance

36. What is never included in the process of valuation?

    A. Comparative Market Analysis
    B. Appraisal
    C. Location
    D. Condition of the house

37. What type of contract allows the parties involved to disaffirm without liability?

    A. Bilateral contract
    B. Implied contract
    C. Unilateral contract
    D. Voidable Contract

38. What fiduciary duty does a broker neglect by failing to disclosing the buyer's inability to afford a down payment?

    A. Obedience
    B. Disclosure
    C. Accountability
    D. Confidentiality

39. James and Peter co-own a property where they both have equal undivided interests and right of survivorship. What co-ownership agreement do they have?

    A. Tenancy in entirety
    B. Joint tenancy
    C. Tenancy in common
    D. Tenancy at will

40. What is an exclusive term to describe the lease entered when an individual buys shares from a housing corporation?

    A. Percentage lease
    B. Gross lease
    C. Net lease
    D. Proprietary lease

41. What is the state of having no legal effect?

    A. Enforceable
    B. Cancelled
    C. Void
    D. Terminated

42. How many square feet constitute an acre?

    A. 25,235
    B. 43,560
    C. 50,525
    D. 70,000

43. What is the set minimum amp for a new construction?

    A. 100 amps
    B. 150 amps
    C. 200 amps
    D. 250 amps

44. What is the debt-to-equity ratio on a mortgage valued at $1,000,000 with a loan of $750,000?

    A. 25%
    B. 50%
    C. 65%
    D. 75%

45. Who controls flood insurance?

    A. FEMA
    B. EPA
    C. CERCLA
    D. FHA

46. What is a detailed building plan that is needed before starting construction?

    A. Building design
    B. Execution plan
    C. Blueprint
    D. Authorized plan

47. What type of house insulation was banned due to the release of formaldehyde fumes?

    A. Foam boards
    B. Loose fill
    C. Vapor barriers
    D. UFFI

48. What is the term used to describe a scenario where an agent represents both the buyer and the seller?

    A. Single agency
    B. Dual agency
    C. Multi agency
    D. Representing both agency

49. Which formal agreement gives an agent the sole right to sell a property?

    A. Purchase agreement
    B. Floating rate
    C. Exclusive Right-to-Sell Agreement
    D. Bridge loan

50. A tenant is legally allowed to remove equipment previously installed to facilitate business operations before the expiry of a lease. Why is this the case?

    A. The equipment is considered trade fixtures
    B. The equipment belongs to the lease holder
    C. The lessor does not want it
    D. It was part of the lease agreement

51. What type of easement attaches rights to an individual rather than the property?

    A. Easement appurtenant
    B. Easement in gross
    C. Prescriptive easement
    D. All of the above

52. What is the name given to the lowest section of the roof that extends into the sidewalls?

    A. Board
    B. Eaves
    C. Joists
    D. Beams

53. Which two parties are responsible for determining the commission earned by the broker?

    A. Seller and agent
    B. Seller and broker
    C. Buyer and agent
    D. Buyer and seller

54. Why must a lawsuit be filed within a specific time after an occurrence?

    A. To prevent the criminal from getting away
    B. Lis pendens
    C. Credibility
    D. Statute of limitations

55. Chris borrows money to purchase a new home and gives the mortgage to the lender as security. What term can be used to refer to Chris?

    A. Mortgagor
    B. Mortgagee
    C. Broker
    D. Buyer

56. What type of lease does a tenant have when he is paying a percentage of gross sales in addition to the base rent?

    A. Proprietary lease
    B. Net lease
    C. Percentage lease
    D. Gross lease

57. Why was the Civil Rights Act of 1866 significant in real estate?

    A. It protected against racial discrimination

    B. It protected interests of women

    C. It protected children's rights

    D. It protected against ageism

58. Why was the Privacy Act of 1974 significant?

    A. It required agencies to publicize records to the Federal Register

    B. It required privacy of records

    C. It required federal government to operate without transparency

    D. It required credit information to be kept private

59. Why was the Fair Housing Act of 1968 significant?

    A. It prohibited agents from asking prospective buyers about income

    B. It prohibited discrimination when selling, financing, or renting of a property

    C. It created affordable housing for low-income citizens

    D. None of the above

60. Jack is trying to convince Mary to sell her property in her neighborhood because it is changing due to the influx of people of other ethnic backgrounds. What is he doing?

    A. Steering

    B. Discriminating

    C. Blockbusting

    D. Convincing

61. What is the name of an agreement that allows for conditions on a property?

    A. Contract

    B. Deed

    C. Lease

    D. Qualified fee estate

62. What is **redlining**?

    A. Refusal by lending institutions to grant loans based on race

    B. Refusal by lending institutions to grant loans to people with poor credit scores

    C. Refusal of lending institutions to grant loans based on the agency being used for a purchase

    D. Refusal of a lending institution to make a loan because the area is integrated or populated by culturally diverse people

63. What is a form of co-ownership that involves a husband and wife having equal and undivided interest in the property?

    A. Joint tenancy

    B. Tenancy in common

    C. Tenancy by entirety

    D. Tenancy at will

64. What is the act of a property reverting to the state on death of the owner?

    A. Escheat

    B. Encumbrance

    C. Easement

    D. Suing

65. If you have a loan of $150,000 with an 8% interest, how much do you pay in interest every month?

    A. $1,000
    B. $1,200
    C. $5,000
    D. $12,000

66. Based on their contract, a lender declares the entire balance of the loan due immediately due to default by the borrower. How is this possible?

    A. Payday loans
    B. Alternative financing
    C. Acceleration clause
    D. Lines of credit

67. What type of payment plan allows a borrower to make smaller payments in the early years of a mortgage with payments increasing over time?

    A. Blanket mortgage
    B. Graduated mortgage
    C. Anomalous mortgage
    D. Balloon mortgage

68. What kind of mortgage should you apply for if you are buying more than an individual unit or plot?

    A. Graduated mortgage
    B. Blanket mortgage
    C. Balloon mortgage
    D. Adjustable rate mortgage

69. A salesperson is presented with two offers on a listed property. One is above the listing price and another below, which offer should he present to the seller?

    A. Both offers
    B. The one above the listing price
    C. The one below the listing price
    D. Neither

70. What is the name of a transaction where a seller finances the whole sale or part of the sale of a property for the buyer?

    A. Mortgage
    B. Refinancing
    C. Purchase money
    D. Buydown

71. What is an assessment of the value of a property as of a specific date based on objective data?

    A. CMA
    B. Listing price
    C. Tax value
    D. Appraisal

72. Which toxic metallic element is found in old paint and water pipes?

    A. Mercury
    B. Manganese
    C. Cadmium
    D. Lead

73. What is the amount of space used to calculate the lease payments which includes the shared property's common and service areas?

    A.   Rentable square footage
    B.   Usable square footage
    C.   Common areas
    D.   Service areas

74. Which chemical compounds commonly used in coolants and refrigeration contribute to the depletion of the ozone?

    A.   CFCs
    B.   Tetrafluoroethane
    C.   Anhydrous ammonia
    D.   Greenhouse gases

75. Which of the following does liability insurance protect you from?

    A.   House fire
    B.   Injury incurred on property
    C.   Flood
    D.   All of the above

76. What is a deed used for?

    A.   To transfer title rights
    B.   An official document proving a bank has loaned money
    C.   A pro forma statement
    D.   A lien

77. What is the measurement used to show the volatility of a market?

    A.   Absorption rate
    B.   Fluctuation rate
    C.   Inflation
    D.   Purchase deviation

78. What is the relationship between a broker and their client called?

    A.   Fiduciary
    B.   Trustee
    C.   Seller disclosure
    D.   Subagent

79. What is the law of agency?

    A.   Commissions that are collected from both parties
    B.   A set of laws that apply to a person who acts on behalf of another person
    C.   The ability to accept an offer on behalf of the seller
    D.   An authorized agency selling another's property

80. A severance is defined as _____.

    A.   Real property that is converted into personal property
    B.   Anything that is attached to the property naturally or by a person
    C.   A person that is acting under a power of attorney
    D.   An agreement between a lender and a borrower in which the borrower pledges collateral on a loan

81. _____ is the increase in value that occurs when combining two parcels into one large parcel.

   A. Redlining
   B. Plottage
   C. Assemblage
   D. Due diligence

82. What is a traffic report?

   A. A. A list of property's a broker is selling at one time
   B. A list of property that have been listed for sale in a specified area
   C. The number of property's a licensed broker is managing
   D. A list of prospects who have inquired or visited the property

83. What is the purpose of the Real Estate Settlement and Procedures Act?

   A. Provide buyers and sellers with disclosures regarding settlement costs
   B. Protect licensed brokers and agents from abusive practices regarding settlements
   C. Ensure buyers and sellers have the ability to back out of settlements within 30 days
   D. Pursue lawsuits against licensed brokers and agents on behalf of the client

84. _____ is also referred to as panic selling or panic peddling.

   A. Redlining
   B. Blockbusting
   C. Amortization
   D. Easement

85. A liability that consists of smaller payments of interest and principal and a balloon payment on the loan maturity date is a _____.

   A. Term loan
   B. Fully amortized loan
   C. Partially amortized loan
   D. Balloon loan

86. When a real estate license is responsible for maintaining a client's property and maximizing the return on investment, the licensee is acting as a _____.

   A. Building manager
   B. Property manager
   C. Broker
   D. Rental agent

87. Which of the following is an example of agricultural real property?

   A. Farm
   B. Warehouse
   C. Condominium building
   D. All of the above

88. A _____ is a law that defines how property in specific geographic area can be used.

   A. National Association of Realtors
   B. Federal Reserve Board
   C. Zoning ordinance
   D. Fair Housing Act

89. What is the purpose of a real estate appraiser?

    A. Provide an estimate of a property's value based on selling price
    B. Provide a professional estimate of the property's market value
    C. Work with a borrower to provide the lender with an annual market value of a home
    D. All of the above

90. _____ measures the rental rates with the value of real property.

    A. Real estate broker
    B. Arbitration
    C. Gross rent multiplier
    D. Mortgagor

91. What is the approach that is used to appraise a home by comparing a property with other properties similar in size and condition in the same area?

    A. Sales approach
    B. Comparison appraisal
    C. Market comparison approach
    D. Market data approach

92. A _____ is a loan where the borrower pays a down payment of 20% and receives a loan of 80%.

    A. Non-conforming loan
    B. Conventional loan
    C. Real property agreement
    D. None of the above

93. A potential buyer has been denied a loan from a lender. The seller of the home allows the buyer to pay an agreed amount every month for ownership of the property. What is this type of agreement called?

  A. Contract for deed
  B. Rent to buy agreement
  C. Real property agreement
  D. None of the above

94. A real estate licensee makes a change to an original contract. They extend the closing date on a contract by 30 days. This change is called a(n) _____.

  A. Assumption
  B. Addendum
  C. Collusion
  D. Reconveyance

95. Which of the following is an example of adverse possession?

  A. A buyer forcibly buying a piece of property
  B. A tenant refusing to leave at the end of a lease
  C. Continuous use of a private road
  D. All of the above

96. Which clause protects an agent from a seller waiting for a listing agreement to end to avoid paying a commission to an agent?

  A. Survival clause
  B. Amendment
  C. Extension clause
  D. Protection clause

97. Which organization is the largest purchaser of home loans in the secondary market and serves to stimulate homeownership?

    A. Mortgage Bankers Association
    B. Federal National Mortgage Association (FNMA)
    C. Government National Mortgage Association
    D. The Mortgage Bank

98. What is the purpose of the U.S. Department of Housing and Urban Development (HUD)?

    A. To ensure everyone has access to fair and equal housing
    B. To provide low income families with home loans
    C. To create government funded homes
    D. To regulate the housing market in the United States

99. Who oversee that Federal Housing Association?

    A. The Senate
    B. Federal National Mortgage Association
    C. U.S. Department of Housing and Urban Development
    D. States

100. The Equal Credit Opportunity Act (ECOA) prohibits lenders from discriminating against _____.

    A. Gender
    B. Marital status
    C. National origin
    D. All of the above

THIS IS THE END OF THE NATIONAL PORTION.

State Portion

1. Which of the following is necessary to become a licensed salesperson?

    A. Pass the salesperson license exam
    B. Have a broker sponsor
    C. Complete the mandated education requirements
    D. All of the above

2. GREC is the acronym for _____.

    A. Georgia Real Estate Commission
    B. Georgia Real Estate Consultancy
    C. General Real Estate Commission
    D. None of the above

3. How do you file a complaint against a salesperson or broker?

    A. Contact the brokerage the agent works for who will then begin the official complaint process
    B. Contact the GREC
    C. Contact the local district court
    D. There is no way to file a complaint

4. Additional education is required if a prospective agent fails the licensing exam _____ times.

    A. 2
    B. 1
    C. 4
    D. 3

5. The _____ was created to protect the public against dishonest licensees and to protect real estate agents from unfair competition.

   A. Real Estate Protections Act
   B. Georgia Real Estate Law of 1925
   C. Georgia Business Protections Act
   D. Real Estate Licensee's Act

6. Which person or group of people upholds the Georgia Real Estate Law?

   A. Georgia State Senate
   B. Georgia Governor
   C. Georgia Real Estate Commission
   D. Local district courts

7. A quorum is made up of _____ commission members.

   A. 5
   B. 4
   C. 10
   D. 2

8. Who is responsible for appointing new commission members when there is a vacancy?

   A. The remaining commission members
   B. A public vote is conducted
   C. Governor
   D. State senate

9. Any person or group may _____ during each commission meeting. GREC will allow 15 minutes for each person or group.

   A. Address complaints against themselves
   B. Request to appear in front of GREC to present an issue
   C. Propose new amendments
   D. None of the above

10. Which of the following can be done by GREC against a licensee who has committed a violation?

    A. Impose a fine
    B. Enforce additional standards of ethics
    C. Issue a cease and desist order
    D. A&C only

11. The GREC has the ability to revoke or suspend a license _____.

    A. After a hearing has occurred
    B. When charges have been brought against the licensee
    C. After failure to fix failures
    D. All of the above

12. If a broker or salesperson's license is revoked, when can they apply for a new license?

    A. After a successful appeal
    B. After 5 years
    C. After 10 years
    D. Immediately after being revoked

13. Georgia courts have the ability to _____ against a person practicing without a license.

    A. Invoke a misdemeanor
    B. Conduct a thorough investigation into transactions conducted by the unlicensed person
    C. Impose jail time
    D. A&C only

14. Which of the following persons cannot conduct real estate transactions without a license?

    A. Brother of a deceased owner
    B. An attorney at law under a duly executed power of attorney
    C. A receiver or trustee of a bankruptcy
    D. Manager of a residential property with the approval of a federal agency

15. A non-licensed real estate assistant has the right to do which of the following?

    A. Show a rental unit and execute a lease
    B. Provide information to a tenant regarding the status of the tenant's security deposit or rent payments
    C. Deliver a lease application
    D. All of the above

16. Which of the following is not a requirement to qualify for a broker or associate broker's license in the state of Georgia?

    A. 18 years of age
    B. Resident of Georgia
    C. Served as a salesperson for 3 years
    D. Provide evidence to complete 60 in class education courses

17. The mandatory post-license education requirement consists of _____.

   A. 20 hours of education
   B. Completion of 3 mandatory and 2 voluntary courses
   C. 25 hours of education
   D. Completion of 2 courses

18. How many years is a commission member's appointment?

   A. 10 years
   B. 5 years
   C. 3 years
   D. There is no term

19. Which of the following information is required on a GREC report?

   A. A summary of the past year
   B. Number of people licensed by GREC
   C. A research and education report which states what was done to further its goal of protecting the public
   D. All of the above

20. Which of the following is requirement of the salesperson license in Georgia?

   A. 21 years of age
   B. A college degree
   C. Evidence of completion of in-class education courses
   D. U.S Citizenship

21. What does it mean to assign a contract?

    A. A brokerage giving a client to a broker
    B. To transfer a contract to another
    C. A seller giving rights to sell to another person
    D. None of the above

22. A person has the right of recission for any reason within _____ under Georgia law.

    A. 3 business days
    B. 5 business days
    C. 10 business days
    D. 2 business days

23. Who is responsible for setting the usury?

    A. The federal government
    B. Lenders
    C. Buyers
    D. The state

24. After closing a homeowner retains a _____ in Georgia

    A. Equitable title
    B. Legal title
    C. Property rights for 60 days
    D. Partial ownership

25. _____ is recognized in the state of Georgia, which allows each owner the right to possess the entire real property.

    A.   Right of survivorship
    B.   Joint tenancy
    C.   Tenancy in common
    D.   Right to possession

26. The _____ limits how much a bank can charge for escrow amounts.

    A.   State government
    B.   Real Estate Settlement Procedures Act
    C.   GREC
    D.   State senator

27. Which of the following is not a requirement to become a community association manager in Georgia?

    A.   A college degree
    B.   18 years of age
    C.   Georgia residency
    D.   High school diploma or equivalent

28. The GREC consists of how many members?

    A.   3
    B.   6
    C.   10
    D.   5

29. Corporation A wants to be granted a license to act as a real estate broker, which of the follow is a requirement?

    A. They must pay addition fees for the licensure
    B. The owner or CEO must have at least a salesperson license
    C. A designated officer needs to be a licensed broker
    D. A designated officer needs to have at least 5 years' experience as a broker

30. Physical possession of property is given to the buyer _____.

    A. When the contract is signed
    B. The day escrow closes
    C. 30 days after escrow
    D. None of the above

31. How is the GREC chairperson appointed?

    A. By the governor
    B. By the commission members
    C. By the public
    D. There is no chairperson

32. A _____ can participate in Georgia real estate transactions in two ways, by referring a client for a fee and by working with a Georgia licensed broker.

    A. Assistants
    B. Attorneys
    C. Out-of-state licensee
    D. None of the above

33. Which of the following is a reason the Georgia governor can remove a commission member?

    A. Incompetence
    B. Neglect of duties
    C. Dishonesty
    D. All of the above

34. Responding to phone inquiries regarding the availability and pricing of brokerage services is an example of _____.

    A. Administrative duties
    B. Commission oversight
    C. Ministerial acts
    D. None of the above

35. Which of the following is true about a salesperson license in Georgia?

    A. They are authorized to engage in real estate activities under a broker's supervision only
    B. They cannot act directly for a principal in a transaction
    C. They can only receive compensation from the sponsoring broker
    D. All of the above

36. Georgia requires a real estate licensee to renew their application every _____.

    A. 6 months
    B. 5 years
    C. 4 years
    D. Year

37. How many hours of continuing education is required when a licensee renews their license?

   A. 30 hours
   B. 24 hours
   C. 50 hours
   D. 100 hours

38. Which of the following is true about an inactive license?

   A. An inactive licensee may complete current real estate activities
   B. The inactive license is held by GREC
   C. An inactive license can only remain inactive for 10 years
   D. All of the above are true

39. Which of the following is not a responsibility of the GREC members?

   A. Evaluate staff operations
   B. Pass real estate laws
   C. Establish a fair qualifying process
   D. All of the above are responsibilities

40. _____ is needed for an out-of-state licensee to obtain a Georgia license without taking the exam.

   A. Reciprocity
   B. 10 years' experience as a broker
   C. A $1,000 fee
   D. All out-of-state licensees must take the exam

41. When a licensee affiliates with a broker, which of the following is required prior to employment?

    A. A written employment agreement must be signed
    B. A non-compete must be signed
    C. A background check must be done
    D. All of the above is required

42. Which of the following is an example of trust funds?

    A. Earnest money
    B. Commission
    C. General operating funds
    D. Referral fees

43. The _____ is responsible for mortgage loan payment when a property is sold subject to debt.

    A. Seller
    B. Buyer
    C. Lender
    D. Brokerage

44. What is the statutory right to redemption after foreclosure in Georgia?

    A. 30 days
    B. 45 days
    C. 1 year
    D. There is no statutory right to redemption

45. What does the Rural Housing Services Administration do?

    A.   Incentivizes housing in rural areas

    B.   Provides land to developers in rural areas

    C.   Guarantees loans on farms and rural homes

    D.   None of the above

46. A lender can legally discriminate in loan terms regarding the applicant's _____.

    A.   Age

    B.   Intent to occupy

    C.   Residency

    D.   All of the above

47. Georgia practices a(n) _____ foreclosure process.

    A.   Judicial

    B.   Non-judicial

    C.   Accelerate

    D.   None of the above

48. Which of the following is the most common reason for disciplinary action in Georgia?

    A.   Unlicensed persons practicing real estate

    B.   Mishandling trust funds

    C.   Lack of broker oversight

    D.   Failure to complete continuing education

49. In Georgia, an unlicensed assistant can do which of the following?

    A. Show property
    B. Host open houses
    C. Cold call
    D. None of the above

50. Which of the following must the brokerage do if a licensee leaves the brokerage?

    A. Brokerage must return the license to the Commission
    B. The broker must return the license to the licensee
    C. The broker must provide the licensee's new brokerage with the license
    D. A&C are true

51. Which statement is true about Brokerage regulations in Georgia?

    A. A brokerage can only have 5 branch offices
    B. A real estate licensee must run each branch office
    C. A broker is required to maintain an office
    D. All of the above are true

52. A licensee must inform the GREC if there is a change in _____.

    A. Mailing address
    B. Residence address
    C. Name
    D. All of the above

THIS IS THE END OF THE STATE PORTION.

Answer Key – National Portion

1.	A	21.	A	41.	C	61.	D	81.	B
2.	B	22.	A	42.	B	62.	D	82.	D
3.	B	23.	B	43.	A	63.	C	83.	A
4.	A	24.	D	44.	D	64.	A	84.	B
5.	D	25.	C	45.	A	65.	A	85.	C
6.	B	26.	C	46.	C	66.	C	86.	B
7.	C	27.	C	47.	D	67.	B	87.	A
8.	D	28.	A	48.	B	68.	B	88.	C
9.	A	29.	D	49.	C	69.	A	89.	B
10.	B	30.	B	50.	A	70.	C	90.	C
11.	B	31.	D	51.	B	71.	D	91.	D
12.	A	32.	A	52.	B	72.	D	92.	B
13.	A	33.	A	53.	B	73.	A	93.	A
14.	C	34.	D	54.	D	74.	A	94.	B
15.	D	35.	A	55.	A	75.	D	95.	C
16.	A	36.	A	56.	C	76.	A	96.	D
17.	B	37.	D	57.	A	77.	A	97.	B
18.	C	38.	B	58.	A	78.	A	98.	A
19.	C	39.	B	59.	B	79.	B	99.	C
20.	D	40.	D	60.	C	80.	A	100.	D

1. **A) A loan that has a predetermined repayment interest rate**

Commonly compared to floating rate, which is a loan that uses external factors as a benchmark for interest rates and is usually fluctuating based on the external market.

2. **B) Civil Rights Act of 1866**

This act declares all citizens equal and under the protection of the law. The law emphasized protecting all citizens of African descent during the Civil War.

3. **B) Promissory note**

This is a financial document by the issuer to the payee that contains a promise to make payment for a definite sum of money. It is usually valid for payment either on demand or on a specified date. It usually contains information regarding the principal amount, interest rate, date and place of issuance, maturity date and signature of the parties involved.

4.   **A) Refinancing**

This is the process of replacing an existing mortgage with another that offers more favorable terms to the borrower. Refinancing enables a borrower to negotiate for lower monthly payments, lower interest rates and renegotiate the loan payment term.

5.   **D) All of the above**

An appurtenance is real property fixed to the land that is passed along with the sale of a property.

6.   **B) Certificate of deposit**

This is a product offered by banks and credit facilities to customers enabling them to deposit a lump sum amount for a predetermined period with an agreed upon interest rate premium. Doing some research on the certificate of deposit terms offered by the different available facilities is important to yield better returns.

7.   **C) $250,000**

$225,000 / (1 - 0.1) = $250,000

8.   **D) Annual percentage rate**

This is the annual rate charged on a loan or investment. It is usually used to express the actual annual cost of funds over the lifespan of a loan or cash investment. As loan arrangements vary among institutions and the situation surrounding the loan, a standardized APR is set to protect borrowers from unreasonably high interest rates.

9.   **A) Public auctions**

Homes are usually put on auction due to default on a mortgage or property taxes. Buying a house at an auction is risky as it often does not give the buyer a chance to view the interior of the house. When buying a property at an auction, it is necessary to run background research on the property.

10.   **B) Pre-qualification**

These is the process of reviewing clients' creditworthiness and is usually used as a marketing strategy to obtain new clients. Creditors usually mail a potential borrower outlining maximum limit for loan.

11. **B) Power of attorney**

This is a legal document that transfers rights to act in place of a principal in the event that they are unable to act for themselves. The terms of the contract usually include what can be managed and where the power of the agent ends.

12. **A) Exclusive listing**

An exclusive listing is an agreement between a seller and an agent stating that commission on a sale can only be earned when a sale is made within a specified period of time. The timeframe for the sale is usually agreed on by both parties while entering the agreement.

13. **A) Single agency**

This is brokerage agreement where a buying agent is assigned the role to represent a buyer and works in single agency capacity as the buyer's agent. This agent is bound by fiduciary duties to the buyer and cannot disclose any confidential information to the other party.

14. **C) Arms-length transaction**

This is a transaction where both the buyer and the seller are acting in self-interest with an aim of getting the better deal. The discrepancy is usually solved when both parties agree on a middle ground that fulfills the interests of both the buyer and the seller.

15. **D) Adjustment date**

This is the changing of a date where calculations on items such as property taxes, rent and damage deposits are done.

16. **A) Assumable mortgage**

This is a mortgage arrangement that allows the seller to transfer the terms and conditions of a mortgage to a buyer. In this case, a buyer absorbs the seller's remaining debt instead of taking out a new mortgage.

17. **B) Call option**

This is a contract signed by both the buyer and the seller giving one party the right to sell and the other the right to buy a property on a future date. The price of the property is usually included in the contract and remains the same regardless of inflation or market shifts.

18. **C) A specified expiration date**

An exclusive listing contract is an agreement where a real estate agent receives commission within a specified amount of time. The agent receives commission no matter how the buyer is found.

19. **C) Reciprocity**

Real estate license reciprocity allows agents to obtain a real estate license in another state by taking the reciprocal state's exam.

20. **D) Privacy**

The 6 fiduciary duties of a real estate agent are: **O**bedience, **L**oyalty, **D**isclosure, **C**onfidentiality, **A**ccountability, and **R**easonable care / diligence (OLDCAR)

21. **A) Conditions that must be met by both the buyer and the seller before closing**

They are set in place to protect the parties involved in the contract. A breach in the contingencies results in the immediate termination of the contract.

22. **A) Any individual whose name appears on the loan document**

This is often someone whose credit score was taken into consideration when determining whether or not a loan can be extended. A co-borrower can be beneficial for a borrower that is unable to get favorable interest rates.

23. **B) Construction loan**

This is a short-term loan that is usually taken to finance the construction of a home or real estate property. It is usually taken to provide cash flow before larger funding is approved.

24. **D) Final walkthrough**

This is a visit done to the property by the buyer after all financing has been secured. A buyer is required to visit the premise and establish whether all the things that were discussed in the contract have been met prior to closing the deal.

25. **C) Fixed mortgage rate**

This is a mortgage loan whose interest rate remains the same throughout the longevity of the loan.

26. **C) Loan to value ratio**

This is defined as the percentage of the home's value owned by the borrower after making a down payment. It is calculated by taking the mortgage loan amount and dividing it by the appraisal value of the property being bought. The higher the loan to value ratio, the less likely lenders are to agree to loans.

27. **C) 20%**

($1,000 * 12) / $60,000 = 0.2

28. **A) Vicarious liability**

This is a secondary form of liability where a superior is held accountable for the actions of his subordinates. In the real estate sector, vicarious liability arises when an agent hired by either the buyer or seller acts inappropriately. In this case, the client is held accountable for the misconduct of his agent.

29. **D) Agency disclosure statement**

This is a statement signed by both the seller and buyer prior to the real estate transaction. Its role is to disclose the role of the agent in the transaction. An agent can either be a broker for either the buyer or the seller, a dual agent or a sub agent. In order to enforce disclosure laws, some states have a disclosure form written into law.

30. **B) Price fixing**

This is a situation that arises where a number of real estate agencies that dominate the market agree on a set commission. Brokers are required by law to set their individual commissions where consideration to the market going rate is allowed. Choosing to agree on a set standard commission could result in the suspension of a broker's license. These laws were set in place to protect the buyers and sellers in the market.

31. **D) IRS**

The IRS uses the general rule that an individual can be classified as an independent contractor if the payer has the right to control the result of work and not how it will be done.

32. **A) Freehold**

Freehold title is a title given to a freehold property where the owner owns the unit and the land on which the establishment has been developed and anything that is erected on the land.

33. **A) $0**

According to the Taxpayer Relief Act of 1997, a married couple is eligible for exemption from capital gain tax on profits of up to $500,000. This can only be claimed provided the property is the primary home of the selling couple meaning they have been living there for at least 2 years. Therefore, Mr. and Mrs. Smith do not owe anything in capital gain tax.

34. **D) Suspended**

He can choose to wait for the suspension to be lifted or look for another broker. A license can be suspended due to violation of insurance laws, providing materially misleading information and fraudulent practices. A revoked can only be reinstated after one year with undeniable evidence of trustworthiness and ability to uphold the law.

35. **A) Umbrella policy**

An umbrella insurance policy is an excess liability policy that is often used as a fail-safe for assets and savings. It is mostly used by people that are at risk of being sued. Contrary to popular belief, an umbrella policy does not cover additional risk area but acts as an addition to an already existing insurance.

36. **A) Comparative Market Analysis**

Comparative Market Analysis is never used in valuation as it is based on the market value of similar properties whereas no two real properties are alike.

37. **D) Voidable Contract**

A voidable contract is a formal agreement between parties that can be rendered obsolete due to legal factors. Some of the factors that can result in a voidable contract being rejected are fraud, undisclosed facts and a breach of the contract. A voidable contract is always considered legal unless rendered unenforceable.

38. **B) Disclosure**

Fiduciary duties arise when an agency operates on behalf of a client. In this case the agent is legally mandated to act in the best interest of the client. When an agent fails to disclose facts that may influence the final decision of the client, he is in violation of the disclosure clause.

39. **B) Joint tenancy**

A joint tenancy is an arrangement where two or more parties agree to co-own a property with equal rights and obligations. Upon death of a partner, the property remains solely in the ownership of the surviving partner. A joint tenancy has to be entered at the same time through a deed. Joint tenancy has the advantage of avoiding legal battles after the demise of a partner but can be hard to settle in the event of a divorced couple.

40. **D) Proprietary lease**

A proprietary lease is a is an agreement that allows a shareholder in a housing corporation to live in a unit equaling their stakes in the corporation. A shareholder does not buy the property but shares in the corporation. In this case, the shares act as collateral on the lease.

41. **C) Void**

This means to be obsolete and have no enforceable terms. Parties to a void contract are not bound by its terms making the contract unenforceable.

42. **B) 43,560**

An acre is a standard unit for measuring land. An acre does not have to be square shaped but contains an equivalent of 43560 square feet.

43. **A) 100 amps**

The minimum is 100 amps as anything below that may not be able to sustain the electric needs of a home. Larger homes can have between 150 and 200 amps based on the type of electronic systems installed. Having a proper electrical distribution in the home will also avoid trips.

44. **D) 75%**

750,000 / 1,000,000 = 0.75

The debt-to-equity ratio is used to determine whether a buyer can afford a house or to refinance an already owned property.

45. **A) FEMA**

The Federal Emergency Management Agency focuses on promoting the need to work together to support citizens and fast respondents. Its goal is to ensure citizens build and sustain to prepare for and recover from calamities.

46. **C) Blueprint**

A blueprint is a reproduction of a technical drawing on a light sensitive sheet that is done using a contact printer. A blueprint is usually required to predetermine the design and pattern that is going to be followed in a construction.

47. **D) UFFI**

Urea Formaldehyde Foam Insulation was used for house insulation in the 70s due to its high thermal resistance. Testing in the lab showed that the insulation produced fumes that were toxic for humans and the environment leading to its ban in 1982.

48. **B) Dual agency**

Dual agency is legal in Pennsylvania provided both the buyer and the seller agree to the arrangement after pros and cons of the relationship are laid on the table. Opting to have a dual agent means that the client cannot expect the agent to act in their best interest as he is representing two conflicting interests.

49.   **C) Exclusive Right-to-Sell Agreement**

This is an agreement between a seller and agent granting the agent or firm the exclusive right to market and sell a property.

50.   **A) The equipment is considered trade fixtures**

Trade fixtures are removable personal property that are installed in a leased space to facilitate business running. For one to be allowed to remove a fixture, it must be essential for the running of the business to not cause damage to the property and be removed before the expiry of the lease.

51.   **B) Easement in gross**

The rights associated by the easement are irrevocable for the person granted. A transfer of the property to another individual through sale or inheritance does not warrant an automatic transfer of the rights to the new owner. This renders the easement of gross void.

52.   **B) Eaves**

An eave is the lower edge of a roof that protrude or hangs over the building's side.

53.   **B) Seller and broker**

The seller and broker are usually responsible for agreeing in the amount of commission that should be paid to the broker

54.   **D) Statute of limitations**

The statute of limitations is a law that sets the maximum period of time parties involved in a rift have to initiate legal proceedings from the day of the occurrence of the event. The time allocated to offences differs according to the nature of the offence.

55.   **A) Mortgagor**

A mortgagor is an individual that borrows money from a lender in order to purchase a property. The lending is based on the individual's credit score and collateral. A title must be handed to the lender as collateral for the loan.

56.   **C) Percentage lease**

A percentage lease is a type of lease where the tenant pays rent plus a percentage of any revenue earned while doing business on the property. This agreement significantly reduces the rent paid. The parties involved agree on a base point where percentage lease kicks in.

57. **A) It protected against racial discrimination**

The Civil Rights act of 1866 banned racial discrimination in real estate and housing transactions. People of any race had equal rights as whites to buy, sell, or lease property.

58. **A) It required agencies to publicize records to the Federal Register**

The Privacy Act of 1974 is an act that established code of fair information maintenance governing the collection, use and maintenance of individuals that is maintained by federal agencies. The act required the agencies to publicize the records in the Federal Register.

59. **B) It prohibited discrimination when selling, financing, or renting of a property**

The 1968 Act prohibited discrimination based on race, religion, national origin, sex, handicap and family status of the sale, financing, and rental of housing.

60. **C) Blockbusting**

This is the act of trying to manipulate tenants to sell or rent their properties at lower rates due to an influx of minority groups in a once segregated neighborhood.

61. **D) Qualified fee estate**

This is an estate agreement that facilitates the grantor to propose a set of conditions. A breach in the condition limitation may result in termination of the agreement. A quality fee estate can also be based on the occurrence of a predetermined event.

62. **D) Refusal of a lending institution to make a loan because the area is integrated or populated by culturally diverse people**

This usually occurs when a lending institution has a map of areas they would not like to initiate credit in. Potential property owners are denied mortgages despite great credit scores due to the location of the property they intend to purchase.

63. **C) Tenancy by entirety**

Only married couples can enter this type of co-ownership where the property is jointly owned as a single entity. It facilitates right of survivorship and can be terminated upon death of spouse or divorce.

64. **A) Escheat**

A property can be reverted to the state if no claimants have come forth to claim the property or the available heir has been deemed legally unfit to be granted ownership. It is revocable once a legal heir claims the property.

65.   **A) $1,000**

($150,000 * 0.08) / 12 = $1,000

66.   **C) Acceleration clause**

This is a contract that allows a lender to require full settlement of an outstanding loan due to a breach of predetermined conditions.

67.   **B) Graduated mortgage**

This is a fixed price loan that allows the borrower to make smaller payments on the loan in the earlier payment years and continues to increase gradually until the mortgage is paid off. It considers individuals who were otherwise not qualified for the higher rate to qualify.

68.   **B) Blanket mortgage**

A blanket mortgage is a mortgage that covers two or more pieces of real estate. The real estate property is held as collateral. Individual properties can be sold without having to retire the mortgage. This insurance is usually taken when purchasing and developing land.

69.   **A) Both offers**

The agent is required by fiduciary duties to present both the offers to the client. Choosing to present the higher offer to the client in order to reap higher commission from the sale is a breach of fiduciary duties.

70.   **C) Purchase money**

This is a mortgage issued by the seller as part of a real estate transaction. This arrangement is usually reached when the buyer is not eligible for the traditional mortgage. A down payment is usually placed on the property as an order of the financial transaction.

71.   **D) Appraisal**

An appraisal is an opinion usually given by a professional on the market value of a property. Properties usually require an appraisal is unique and market value of similar properties may not offer an accurate value of the property.

72.   **D) Lead**

Lead is a periodic metal that was used in paint in the 1970s as it accelerated drying, maintained a fresh appearance and resisted moisture. Older plumbing systems used lead lines and water often corroded the material as it was transported to the consumer's taps. Use of lead in paint was discontinued as it was found to cause nervous system damage and stunted growth in children.

73. **A) Rentable square footage**

Rentable square footage is inclusive of the usable square footage and common areas. The price per rentable square foot is usually calculated using a pro-rata calculation based on the size of the space being leased.

74. **A) CFCs**

CFCs are nonflammable chemicals that are commonly used in aerosol sprays and industrial cleaning products. Once these chemicals are released into the atmosphere they rise into the stratosphere where ultraviolet rays from the sun break them down. This breakdown releases chlorine atoms that destroy ozone molecules therefore forming ozone holes.

75. **D) All of the above**

Liability insurance covers everything from house fires, injuries incurred on the property, floods, injured domestic workers, falling trees, and more.

76. **A) To transfer title rights**

The buyer and seller must both sign a deed to transfer the property's ownership.

77. **A) Absorption rate**

This is a ration of the number of properties that have been sold against the number of properties that are available for sale within a specified area.

78. **A) Fiduciary**

Fiduciary is the relationship between client and broker. An agent is the fiduciary of the client.

79. **B) A set of laws that apply to a person who acts on behalf of another person**

The law of agency is a set of duties that real estate professionals owe to their clients, including disclosures that must be made to the client. These duties are set by each state.

80. **A) Real property that is converted into personal property**

There are two types of severance, actual severance and constructive severance. An actual severance is when an item is removed from the land and a constructive severance is when an item is detached by intent.

81. **B) Plottage**

Plottage occurs when the total value of a combined parcel is worth more than the sum of the individual parcels. The process of combining the parcel is called assemblage.

82. **D) A list of prospects who have inquired or visited the property**

A traffic report keeps a count of prospective buyers who have called about or visited the property.

83. **A) Provide buyers and sellers with disclosures regarding settlement costs**

RESPA is a consumer protection act that provides procedures that need to be followed in one-to-four residential real estate sales. It assists in eliminating abusive practices during settlements, bars kickback and limits the use of escrow accounts

84. **B) Blockbusting**

An illegal act that is not permitted by the Fair Housing Laws. This method manipulates homeowners into selling or renting their home at a lower price by falsely stating that minorities (racial, religious, etc.,) are moving into a once segregated neighborhood.

85. **C) Partially amortized loan**

A partially amortized loan is a loan that involves partial amortization during the loan term and a lump sum on the loan maturity date.

86. **B) Property manager**

A property manager is responsible for maintaining a client's property and maximizing the return on the client's investment. When a licensee acts on behalf of a client and doing the above, they are acting as a property manager.

87. **A) Farm**

A farm is an example of an agricultural real property. Agricultural real property is property that is used for farming and can be the farmers real presence.

88. **C) Zoning ordinance**

A zoning ordinance specifies which zones can be used for residential or commercial purposes. It may also regulate the lot size, placement, bulk and height of the structures.

89. **B) Provides a professional estimate of the property's market value**

A real estate appraiser is responsible for providing an estimate of a property's market value. This is established by using appraisal methods and a trained, professional judgement.

90. **C) Gross rent multiplier**

The gross rent multiplier is the ratio of the price of an investment property to its annual rental income. This ratio is prior to accounting for expenses like insurance, utilities, and property taxes.

91. **D) Market data approach**

The market data approach, also called sales comparison approach, finds value of property by comparing it to other properties that are similar in size and condition. The properties are also in the same area. Appraisers will typically use comparable homes that were sold within 6 months of the appraisal.

92. **B) Conventional loan**

In a conventional loan a borrower pays a down payment of 20% and receives a loan for the remaining 80%. There is not government involvement in a conventional loan.

93. **A) Contract for deed**

A contract for deed or an installment contract is a simpler way for a buyer to buy a home. It is an agreement between the seller and the buyer that the buyer will pay a monthly payment to the seller and the deed to the home is turned over to the buyer when all payments have been made.

94. **B) Addendum**

An addendum is a change made to an original contract. The addendum is also called an amendment.

95. **C) Continuous use of a private road**

Adverse possession allows a person to claim a property right owned by another person. The person can gain the title by using another's property continuously, openly and without permission for a certain period of time. It is also called squatter's rights.

96. **D) Protection clause**

This clause entitles a real estate broker to a commission after the listing is expired or canceled. It is only valid if buyers have viewed the property.

97. **B) Federal National Mortgage Association (FNMA)**

The FNMA is a government sponsored enterprise that serves to stimulate homeownership. It is the largest purchaser of home loans and raises money to buy notes from lenders.

98.   **A) To ensure everyone has access to fair and equal housing**

HUD is tasked with providing housing and community development assistance, and ensure everyone has access to fair and equal housing. The mission is to create strong, sustainable and inclusive communities and provide quality and affordable homes to everyone.

99.   **C) U.S. Department of Housing and Urban Development**

The FHA provides mortgage insurance on loans that are made by FHA approved lenders. They insure single family homes, multi-family properties, hospitals and residential care facilities.

100.   **D) All of the above**

The ECOA prohibits discrimination in lending due to race, color, sex, religion, marital status, national origin and age.

Answer Key – State Portion

#		#		#	
1.	D	21.	B	41.	A
2.	A	22.	A	42.	A
3.	B	23.	D	43.	A
4.	D	24.	A	44.	D
5.	B	25.	C	45.	C
6.	C	26.	B	46.	B
7.	B	27.	A	47.	B
8.	C	28.	B	48.	B
9.	B	29.	C	49.	D
10.	D	30.	B	50.	D
11.	A	31.	B	51.	C
12.	C	32.	C	52.	D
13.	D	33.	D		
14.	A	34.	C		
15.	D	35.	D		
16.	A	36.	C		
17.	C	37.	B		
18.	B	38.	B		
19.	D	39.	B		
20.	C	40.	A		

1. **D) All of the above**

Georgia requires all of the above for a person to become a licensed real estate person.

2. **A) Georgia Real Estate Commission**

The GREC Is a regulating body that is responsible for regulating the brokerage industry and licensing real estate practitioners in the state of Georgia.

3. **B) Contact the GREC**

To file a complaint against a broker or salesperson, the client must file a complaint with GREC. The E-1 form is used to file this complaint.

4. **D) 3**

If a person fails their license exam 3 times, the state requires the person to complete additional education.

5. **B) Georgia Real Estate Law of 1925**

    This law was created to protect the public against dishonest and incompetent licensees and protect licensees against unfair competition. It also lays out a list of standards licensees are expected to abide by.

6. **C) Georgia Real Estate Commission**

    GREC is responsible for upholding the Georgia Real Estate law, which requires licensees to abide by listed standards and protect both the public and the licensees.

7. **B) 4**

    A quorum means that there are enough of the commission's members present to carry out business.

8. **C) Governor**

    The governor has the responsibility to appoint a new member of the GREC if there is a vacancy.

9. **B) Request to appear in front of the GREC to present an issue**

    Any person or group may make a written request to appear before the GREC. GREC will allow 3 people or groups to present an issue with 15 mins allotted each per meeting.

10. **D) A&C only**

    The commission has the ability to impose a fine not exceeding $1,000 per violation, for each day the same violation is practiced and issue a cease and desist order.

11. **A) After a hearing has occurred**

    The GREC has the ability to suspend or revoke a real estate license but can only do it after a hearing has occurred. This is only done for the most serious of violations.

12. **C) After 10 years**

    After the GREC has revoked a license the person must wait 10 years before they are able to reapply for the license.

13. **D) A&C only**

    The courts are capable of imposing a jail sentence or convict as a misdemeanor. The GREC can also impose a cease and desist order or a fine.

14.   **A) Brother of a deceased owner**

The brother of a deceased owner does not have the ability to sell a home without a license. Others who do not need a license includes a licensed certified public account acting as an incident to the practice of public accounting.

15.   **D) All of the above**

They can also perform ministerial acts explicitly authorized by a broker, in writing and provide broker authorized information regarding a rental unit, lease application and/or a lease. The have the right to receive a lease application, lease, security deposit, rental payment, or other related payment. They can provide information to an owner regarding financial accounts and payments from the owner's tenants.

16.   **A) Be 18 years of age**

A broker must be 21 years of age or older. They must also have a high school degree or equivalent and pass the real estate examination.

17.   **C) 25 hours of education**

The evidence of completion of coursework and submission must be submitted to the GREC within one year of licensure.

18.   **B) 5 years**

GREC commissioner member terms are 5 years long. Only one license term can expire per year. The Governor is responsible for appointing commissioners.

19.   **D) All of the above**

The report must also include a list of staff, plans for the coming year about research and education and a financial report that shows the income and disbursement of funds. The report is provided to the Governor and both houses of the General Assembly.

20.   **C) Evidence of completion of in-class education courses**

A salesperson only needs to be 18 years of age, have a high school diploma or its equivalent and have a Georgia residency. They must also pass an examination that has been administered and approved by the Commission.

21.   **B) To transfer the contract to another**

This occurs when one party who has real estate under contract passes or assigns the rights of the contract to another party. This is commonly used in real estate contracts to "flip" real estate without having capital coming out of your pocket.

22.   **A) 3 business days**

A recission is the cancellation of a real estate contract between the buyer and the seller. Georgia law gives the buyer and the seller 3 business days to rescind a real estate contract for any reason.

23.   **D) The state**

Ceilings for maximum interest rates that lenders may charge are set by the state. Any rate set above that ceiling is considered usurious and illegal. The current maximum usury rate in Georgia is 60%.

24.   **A) Equitable title**

An equitable title is the person's right to obtain full ownership of a property or property interest.

25.   **C) Tenancy in common**

Tenancy in common is the right to possess the entire real property even if ownership interest is not equal. Each ownership can also be sold, mortgaged, or willed to another separately.

26.   **B) Real Estate Settlement Procedures Act**

The RESPA is a federal law enacted by congress that provides cost disclosures. It was created to help eliminate abusive practices in real estate settlement processes, limit the use of escrow accounts and prohibit kickbacks.

27.   **A) A college degree**

A college degree is not necessary to become a community association manager. The community association manager acts on behalf of a broker providing community management services only.

28.   **B) 6**

The GREC consists of 6 members who have 5-year terms and cannot have terms ending at the same time.

29.   **C) A designated officer needs to be a licensed broker**

The company must have a designated officer who is a licensed broker in order to be granted the broker license.

30. **B) The day escrow closes**

Escrow is the use of a 3rd party that holds an asset or fund before it is transferred from one party to another. This is the day when a buyer officially becomes the owner of property.

31. **B) By the commission members**

Commission members are responsible for appointing their own chairperson. A chairperson is appointed on a yearly basis.

32. **C) Out-of-state licensee**

Out-of-state licensees are able to refer a client for a fee as long as no brokerage services are provided and can work with a Georgia broker on a single transaction under a written agreement.

33. **D) All of the above**

Neglect of duties, incompetence and dishonest are all reasons a governor can remove a commission member. Another reason is the inability to perform the necessary duties.

34. **C) Ministerial acts**

These acts are things that can be done by a licensee that are informative in nature. They are brokerage activities that do not require discretion or the exercise of the licensee's own judgement.

35. **D) All of the above**

All of the listed is true about a salesperson's license. They must work under a broker; they cannot work directly for a principal and can only receive compensation from a broker.

36. **C) 4 years**

The licensee must renew their license every 4 years at the end of their birthday month. A renewal fee and proof of completion of continuing education is required.

37. **B) 24 hours**

There is a total of 24 hours of continuing education that is required by the state of Georgia.

38. **B) The inactive license is held by GREC**

The licensee cannot engage in any real estate activities and the license can remain inactive indefinitely. A license which has been inactive for 2 or more years requires continuing education in order to activate.

39.　**B) Pass real estate laws**

Passing real estate laws is not a responsibility of the commission. Other responsibilities include developing a spirit of cooperation and unity among commission members, establishing a fair and unbiased hearing process, and communicating with the industry and the public.

40.　**A) Reciprocity**

This is also called mutual recognition and is an agreement between states that allow you to get a license in another state.

41.　**A) A written employment agreement must be signed**

Both parties need to sign an agreement which outlines compensations during employment, compensation for unfinished transactions when leaving the brokerage and what listings and clients the licensee can take with them when they leave the brokerage.

42.　**A) Earnest money**

Earnest money is money held by the brokerage as intent to buy property. It is held until closing and is then applied towards the buyer's down payment and closing costs. If the buyer fails to close the contract, then the seller is able to keep the earnest money.

43.　**A) Seller**

A seller is responsible for repayment when there is a mortgage still left on a home when it is sold.

44.　**D) There is no statutory right of redemption**

Once a home has been foreclosed it cannot be redeemed, it must be sold back to the original owners.

45.　**C) Guarantees loans on farms and rural homes**

This is a public agency that provides loans on farms and rural homes. It has programs specifically for a farm operation.

46.　**B) Intent to occupy**

A borrower's intent to occupy can affect the loan terms for a property requiring a mortgage.

47.　**B) Non-judicial**

A non-judicial foreclosure is a foreclosure that does not have to go through the court process. A lender can foreclose on property without filing a suit or appearing in court.

48.   **B) Mishandling trust funds**

This is the most common reason for disciplinary action. Trust funds are money or valuables that have been temporarily entrusted to a broker by a client or customer.

49.   **D) None of the above**

An unlicensed assistant cannot do any of the above. They also cannot answer questions regarding a listing or handle trust funds.

50.   **D) A&C are true**

Both are true and a brokerage must do one or the other. If the license has been released to the Commission the licensee has 30 days to affiliate with a new brokerage or switch to an inactive status.

51.   **C) A broker is required to maintain an office**

A broker must have an office and if the location of the office changes, then the broker needs to notify the Commission within 30 days. A broker is also allowed to have an unlimited number of branches and the branch offices do not need to be run by a real estate licensee.

52.   **D) All of the above**

Licensee's must notify the GREC if there is a change in mailing address, residence address or name. This must be done within one month of the change and must be done for inactive licenses as well.

Practice Test 2

Directions:

1.   You have a 4-hour time limit to complete the whole exam.

2.   To pass, aim to answer at least 75 out of 100 questions correctly on the national portion **AND** at least 39 out of 52 questions on the state portion.

3.   Some questions will require mathematics. You may use a calculator.

4.   **Phones and pagers are not allowed. Having either will result in automatic dismissal from the exam and nullification of exam scores.**

Tips:

- Answer all questions even if you are unsure.
- Mark any questions you are stuck on and revisit them after you are done. The exam is timed so make sure you finish as many questions as you can.
- After reading the question, try answering it in your head first to avoid getting confused by the choices.
- Read the entire question before looking at the answers.
- Use the process of elimination to filter out choices that don't seem correct to increase your chances of selecting the correct answer.
- Be aware of important keywords like **not, sometimes, always,** and **never**. These words completely alter the ask of the question so it's important to keep track of them.

PLEASE READ THESE INSTRUCTIONS CAREFULLY.

59

Name: _____

NATIONAL PORTION

Date: _____

1. Ⓐ Ⓑ ● Ⓓ
2. ● Ⓑ Ⓒ Ⓓ
3. Ⓐ Ⓑ Ⓒ ●
4. ● Ⓑ Ⓒ Ⓓ
5. Ⓐ Ⓑ ● Ⓓ
6. Ⓐ ● Ⓒ Ⓓ
7. ● Ⓑ Ⓒ Ⓓ
8. Ⓐ Ⓑ ● Ⓓ
9. Ⓐ Ⓑ ● Ⓓ
10. A Ⓐ ● Ⓒ Ⓓ
11. Ⓐ Ⓑ ● Ⓓ
12. Ⓐ Ⓑ ● Ⓓ
13. ● Ⓑ Ⓒ Ⓓ
14. ● Ⓑ Ⓒ Ⓓ
15. ● Ⓑ Ⓒ Ⓓ
16. B ● Ⓑ Ⓒ Ⓓ
17. Ⓐ ● Ⓒ Ⓓ
18. C Ⓐ Ⓑ Ⓒ ●
19. Ⓐ Ⓑ ● Ⓓ
20. ● Ⓑ Ⓒ Ⓓ
21. Ⓐ Ⓑ Ⓒ ●
22. ● Ⓑ Ⓒ Ⓓ
23. Ⓐ Ⓑ ● Ⓓ
24. Ⓐ Ⓑ Ⓒ ●
25. Ⓐ Ⓑ Ⓒ ●
26. A Ⓐ ● Ⓒ Ⓓ
27. ● Ⓑ Ⓒ Ⓓ
28. ● Ⓑ Ⓒ Ⓓ
29. B Ⓐ Ⓑ Ⓒ ●
30. A Ⓐ Ⓑ ● Ⓓ

31. B Ⓐ Ⓑ Ⓒ ●
32. A Ⓐ Ⓑ Ⓒ ●
33. Ⓐ ● Ⓒ Ⓓ
34. Ⓐ ● Ⓒ Ⓓ
35. A Ⓐ ● Ⓒ Ⓓ
36. Ⓐ ● Ⓒ Ⓓ
37. Ⓐ ● Ⓒ Ⓓ
38. Ⓐ Ⓑ ● Ⓓ
39. Ⓐ Ⓑ ● Ⓓ
40. B Ⓐ Ⓑ Ⓒ ●
41. B ● Ⓑ Ⓒ Ⓓ
42. ● Ⓑ Ⓒ Ⓓ
43. A Ⓐ Ⓑ ● Ⓓ
44. Ⓐ Ⓑ ● Ⓓ
45. Ⓐ Ⓑ Ⓒ ●
46. ● Ⓑ Ⓒ Ⓓ
47. Ⓐ Ⓑ Ⓒ ●
48. ● Ⓑ Ⓒ Ⓓ
49. Ⓐ Ⓑ ● Ⓓ
50. Ⓐ Ⓑ Ⓒ ●
51. Ⓐ ● Ⓒ Ⓓ
52. Ⓐ ● Ⓒ Ⓓ
53. Ⓐ ● Ⓒ Ⓓ
54. Ⓐ ● Ⓒ Ⓓ
55. Ⓐ ● Ⓒ Ⓓ
56. Ⓐ Ⓑ Ⓒ Ⓓ
57. B Ⓐ Ⓑ ● Ⓓ
58. ● Ⓑ Ⓒ Ⓓ
59. D Ⓐ Ⓑ ● Ⓓ
60. C Ⓐ ● Ⓒ Ⓓ

61. Ⓐ Ⓑ Ⓒ ●
62. Ⓐ ● Ⓒ Ⓓ
63. Ⓐ Ⓑ ● Ⓓ
64. Ⓐ Ⓑ ● Ⓓ
65. Ⓐ ● Ⓒ Ⓓ
66. A Ⓐ ● Ⓒ Ⓓ
67. ● Ⓑ Ⓒ Ⓓ
68. ● Ⓑ Ⓒ Ⓓ
69. Ⓐ Ⓑ ● Ⓓ
70. A Ⓐ Ⓑ Ⓒ ●
71. Ⓐ Ⓑ ● Ⓓ
72. Ⓐ ● Ⓒ Ⓓ
73. ● Ⓑ Ⓒ Ⓓ
74. Ⓐ ● Ⓒ Ⓓ
75. B ● Ⓑ Ⓒ Ⓓ
76. ● Ⓑ Ⓒ Ⓓ
77. Ⓐ ● Ⓒ Ⓓ
78. Ⓐ Ⓑ Ⓒ ●
79. Ⓐ Ⓑ ● Ⓓ
80. Ⓐ ● Ⓒ Ⓓ
81. ● Ⓑ Ⓒ Ⓓ
82. C Ⓐ Ⓑ Ⓒ ●
83. P Ⓐ ● Ⓒ Ⓓ
84. ● Ⓑ Ⓒ Ⓓ
85. B ● Ⓑ Ⓒ Ⓓ
86. N Ⓐ Ⓑ ● Ⓓ
87. Ⓐ Ⓑ ● Ⓓ
88. A Ⓐ ● Ⓒ Ⓓ
89. Ⓐ Ⓑ ● Ⓓ
90. B Ⓐ ● Ⓒ Ⓓ

91. A Ⓐ Ⓑ ● Ⓓ
92. Ⓐ ● Ⓒ Ⓓ
93. B Ⓐ Ⓑ ● Ⓓ
94. C Ⓐ Ⓑ Ⓒ ●
95. Ⓐ ● Ⓒ Ⓓ
96. ● Ⓑ Ⓒ Ⓓ
97. Ⓐ Ⓑ Ⓒ ●
98. ● Ⓑ Ⓒ Ⓓ
99. B Ⓐ Ⓑ ● Ⓓ
100. ● Ⓑ Ⓒ Ⓓ

National Portion

1. What is the process of attempting to recover a loan from a borrower that has stopped making payments?

   A. Concession
   B. Final walk through
   C. Foreclosure
   D. Private mortgage insurance

2. What fibrous material causes cancer when released into the air?

   A. Asbestos
   B. Cotton
   C. Textiles
   D. Trunks

3. What are the vertical beams that frame the house?

   A. Frames
   B. Joists
   C. Shingles
   D. Studs

4. What is a reason a broker may be suspended or have their license revoked?

   A. Misrepresentation
   B. Failure to retain clients
   C. Failure to sell property within specified timeframe
   D. None of the above

5. A property manager makes routine rounds to repair air conditioning vents. What is the term used to refer to this?

   A. Aesthetic maintenance
   B. Avoiding depreciation
   C. Preventive maintenance
   D. Proration

6. What is another term that can be used to refer to the lender?

   A. Seller
   B. Mortgagee
   C. Mortgagor
   D. Loanee

7. If a seller nets $150,000 from the sale of her home, and the commission is 4%, how much did the home sell for?

   A. $144,000
   B. $148,500
   C. $156,000
   D. $156,250

8. What is the name given to the restriction of land usage by the local authorities?

   A. Building codes
   B. Denial
   C. Land zoning
   D. Property tax

9. What is the lender required to do once it is a borrower is unable to clear a mortgage?

   A. Threaten borrower
   B. Sell property without court order
   C. Initiate judicial foreclosure
   D. Evict the borrower

10. Which association represents title insurance?

   A. American Land Title Association
   B. CERCLA
   C. Fair Housing Act
   D. FEMA

11. Which law was passed to regulate credit bureaus?

   A. Annuity law
   B. Consumer credit law
   C. Fair Credit Reporting Act
   D. Truth in Lending Act

12. What is the legal right granted to exit a property?

   A. Easement
   B. Escheat
   C. Right of egress
   D. Right of ingress

13. What is the name given to non-monetary investment?

   A. Sweat equity
   B. Investment
   C. Capital
   D. Maintenance

14. What type of arrangement allows a borrower to negotiate a lower interest rate?

   A. Buydown
   B. Mortgage
   C. Purchase money
   D. Purchase price

15. What is a title without any lien?

   A. Clear title
   B. Deed
   C. Freehold
   D. Regular title

16. What is the name given to the breakdown of an individual's credit history?

   A. Credit assessment
   B. Credit report
   C. Financial record
   D. Repayment report

17. What is another term used to describe ownership?

A. Credit
B. Equity
C. Liability
D. Shares

18. What is the notice filed against a borrower on missing the repayment deadline?

A. Notice of cessation
B. Notice to cure
C. Notice of default
D. Notice of intention

19. What is the name given to describe the period a lender must keep a loan offer open to the borrower?

A. Due diligence period
B. Loan repayment period
C. Lock-in period
D. Target hold period

20. Which of the following is a lease break?

A. When a tenant breaks a rent prior to the date of expiry without a legal reason
B. When a tenant terminates a contract once the lease has expired
C. When a tenant breaks a lease with the agreement of the landlord
D. When a landlord allows a tenant to sublease his residence

21. What is the term used to refer to a situation where the amount of funds required to meet an obligation are **not** available?

A. Buydown
B. Debt to income ratio
C. Escrow
D. Shortfall

22. What is the term used to describe a situation where taxes are reduced or completely scrapped to increase buyers in the market?

A. Tax abatement
B. Tax exemption
C. Tax evasion
D. Duty free

23. A property originally assessed at $500,000 appreciated at 4% the first year and then 5% the year after. What is its current value?

A. $525,000
B. $545,000
C. $546,000
D. None of the above

24. Which entity performs the percolation test?

A. Department of State
B. Building Inspector
C. Homeowners Association
D. Department of Health

25. If a property is taxed at 25% with a tax levy of $92,000, what is its assessed value?

- A. $65,000
- B. $115,000
- C. $122,666
- D. $368,000

26. What is the name given to a brief summary of the history of a title?

- A. Abstract of title
- B. Chain of title
- C. Deed chain
- D. History of deed

27. What material is used in construction to cover joints where two or more types of materials meet?

- A. Flashing
- B. Metal
- C. Wood
- D. Joint

28. What is the lowest section of the roof that overhangs beyond the sidewalls of the building?

- A. Eaves
- B. Joists
- C. Stud
- D. Shingles

29. Which real estate metric is found by dividing cash flow by the deposit and settlement costs?

- A. Cash out
- B. Cash on cash return
- C. Lock in period
- D. Loan to value ratio

30. Which board committee is responsible for maintaining the aesthetic view of a town?

- A. Architectural Review Board
- B. Federal government
- C. Municipality
- D. HOA

31. What type of lease is taken on a loft?

- A. Net lease
- B. Gross lease
- C. Percentage lease
- D. Proprietary lease

32. What clause can prohibit having loud parties?

- A. House rules
- B. Regulations
- C. Lease terms
- D. Noise permit

33. What is the measurement used to show the volatility of a market?

   A. Fluctuation rate
   B. Absorption rate
   C. Inflation
   D. Purchase deviation

34. What is the mortgage clause that allows a lender the right to demand immediate payment of a mortgage?

   A. Cancellation clause
   B. Acceleration clause
   C. Prepayment Penalty clause
   D. Release clause

35. Which agreement allows a property holder to cross another person's land?

   A. Easement appurtenant
   B. Easement in gross
   C. Prescriptive easement
   D. None of the above

36. Which of the following is insurance taken out as a protection against malfunctions associated with the acquisition of a new home?

   A. Flood insurance
   B. Homeowner's warranty insurance
   C. HO2
   D. Hazard insurance

37. What is it called when someone takes possession of a property without being the actual title holder?

   A. Acceleration clause
   B. Adverse possession
   C. Easement
   D. Escheat

38. What is a non-possessory interest in property or restrictive covenant burdening the title?

   A. Adverse possession
   B. Easement
   C. Encumbrance
   D. Escheat

39. What is the name given to the long beams that span the piers of a foundation offering support to the floor or ceiling?

   A. Eaves
   B. Frames
   C. Joists
   D. Studs

40. What conveys a grantor's interest in real property?

   A. Agreement
   B. Conveyance
   C. Offering the loan
   D. Title

41. What prohibits the solicitation of residential property listings?

    A. Commingling
    B. Non-solicitation order
    C. Regulation Z
    D. Termination of tenancy

42. What is exempt from property taxation?

    A. Colleges
    B. Office buildings
    C. Supermarkets
    D. Unoccupied land

43. Which fiduciary duty is violated by commingling?

    A. Accountability
    B. Disclosure
    C. Obedience
    D. Loyalty

44. What gives the government power to appropriate private property?

    A. Right of first refusal
    B. Riparian rights
    C. Eminent domain
    D. None of the above

45. What is the owner of a building prohibited to do regarding the disabled?

    A. Allow the disabled to be tenants
    B. Make the building accessible to the disabled
    C. Ensure they are treated like other tenants
    D. Refuse modifications for handicapped tenants

46. What act prohibits discrimination based on disability?

    A. The Americans with Disabilities Act of 1990
    B. Fair Housing Act
    C. Civil Rights Act of 1866
    D. Civil Right Act of 1964

47. What is the name given to a property tenure that can be terminated at any time?

    A. Tenancy in sufferance
    B. Terminated tenancy
    C. Tenancy in common
    D. Tenancy at will

48. If you have a loan of $350,000 with a 7% interest, how much do you pay in interest every month?

    A. $2,041
    B. $2,260
    C. $27,125
    D. $31,208

49. What law prohibits any type of discrimination on the basis of sex and gender?

    A.   Fair Housing Act
    B.   Civil Rights Act of 1866
    C.   Civil Rights Act Amendment of 1974
    D.   Americans with Disabilities Act

50. In 1988, the Civil Rights Act was amended to include?

    A.   Married women
    B.   Immigrants
    C.   Black people
    D.   Handicaps and familial status

51. What is the net income of a property valued at $500,000 and a capitalization rate of 14%?

    A. $70,000
    B. $43,000
    C. $840,000
    D.   None of the above

52. What is the name of an appointed official who estimates the value of real property for taxing purposes?

    A.   Agent
    B.   Assessor
    C.   Appraiser
    D.   Tax official

53. What is the term used to describe a situation where a mortgage balance decreases due to periodic installments that pay down the principal and interest?

    A.   Adjustable-rate mortgage
    B.   Amortization
    C.   Lock-in period
    D.   Fixed-rate mortgage

54. What is an annual tax levied on the value of real property?

    A.   Capital gains tax
    B.   Real estate tax
    C.   Progressive tax
    D.   Regressive tax

55. What is the name given to a situation where an individual uses borrowed money to purchase a property?

    A.   Buydown
    B.   Purchase money
    C.   Leverage
    D.   Shorting

56. Which air conditioning system facilitates both heating and cooling?

    A.   Forced air system
    B.   Cooling system
    C.   Heating system
    D.   Thermostat

57. What is the waiting time for a real estate agent to renew a license once it is revoked?

    A. Two months
    B. One year
    C. Five years
    D. It is never reinstated

58. Who manages a co-op?

    A. Board of directors
    B. CEO
    C. Co-op developers
    D. Tenants

59. What is the value estimating process that uses similar available properties to determine the value of land?

    A. Mirror method
    B. Sales comparison method
    C. Allocation method
    D. Abstraction method

60. Who is required to sign a deed in a real estate transaction?

    A. Attorney
    B. Buyer
    C. Grantor
    D. Lender

61. What is a poisonous gas that comes from the breakdown of minerals in soil?

    A. Ammonia
    B. Chlorine
    C. Helium
    D. Radon

62. What are the rights of a person whose property is adjacent to or crossed by a river?

    A. Exclusive rights to sell
    B. Riparian rights
    C. Rights of first refusal
    D. Right of disclosure

63. What law requires full disclosure of all credit terms for consumer loans under the Truth in Lending Act?

    A. Americans with Disabilities Act
    B. Civil Rights Act
    C. Fair Housing Act
    D. Regulation Z

64. What is the name given to granting priority to an individual to buy or lease a property?

    A. Bundle of rights
    B. Exclusive right to sell
    C. Right of first refusal
    D. Right of possession

65. What is the loss of property value caused by economic or functional factors?

   A. Economic obsolescence
   B. Depreciation
   C. Legal obsolescence
   D. Aesthetic obsolescence

66. What kind of agent is a real estate agent?

   A. Special agent
   B. General agent
   C. Dual agent
   D. Subagent

67. What valuing method is Comparative Market Analysis **not** considered as?

   A. Appraisal
   B. Home valuing
   C. Depreciation valuing
   D. Tax returns valuing

68. What is a specific lien claimed by someone who has performed construction / repair / renovation work on the property and has **not** been paid?

   A. Mechanic's lien
   B. Involuntary lien
   C. Mortgage
   D. Judicial lien

69. What is the bottom piece of a frame that provides a nailing surface for the floor and wall system?

   A. Eaves
   B. Joist
   C. Sill plate
   D. Stud

70. What is a broker allowed to purchase for a real estate salesperson?

   A. Phone
   B. Medical insurance cover
   C. Retirement plan
   D. A company vehicle

71. When does a real estate salesperson first provide the agency disclosure form?

   A. When the deal is about to be closed
   B. After closing the deal
   C. First substantial contact
   D. Never

72. What is the definition of steering?

   A. When you knowingly provide inaccurate information
   B. Guiding families with children into an apartment building with other families with children and away from other buildings
   C. Discriminating against people due to socio-economic status
   D. Failing to provide proof of continuing real estate education

73. What is the value of a point on a mortgage?

    A.   1% of loan
    B.   5% of the loan
    C.   10% of the loan
    D.   50% of the loan

74. What type of talent are real estate salespeople?

    A.   Assistants
    B.   Independent contractors
    C.   Part time employees
    D.   Full time employees

75. What is the term used to describe a building that is separate from the main house?

    A.   Supplemental structure
    B.   Accessory building
    C.   Secondary land
    D.   Shed

76. The estate that provides absolute ownership of land is called?

    A.   Fee simple estate
    B.   Life estate
    C.   Conditional fee estate
    D.   Legal life estate

77. Which of the following is an example of community property?

    A.   Property that is inherited by the husband through marriage
    B.   Income that is earned by one spouse during the marriage
    C.   Income earned prior to marriage
    D.   A gift given to one spouse during the marriage

78. Fixture are considered _____.

    A.   Hypothecation
    B.   An agreement between the two parties
    C.   Items that are removable by the tenant before the expiration date of the lease
    D.   Real property

79. The commission that is due to a salesperson is decided by?

    A.   Chattels
    B.   State Law
    C.   Mutual Agreement
    D.   Court Decree

80. A real estate broker has become an agent of the seller when ____.

    A.   A listing agreement with the seller has been executed
    B.   They are responsible for sharing commissions
    C.   A broker acts in good faith
    D.   They are procuring cause

81. What is a promissory note?

 A. An agreement between the mortgage company and borrower that shows the terms of the loan
 B. A document that states the buyer's intention to buy a property for a specified amount
 C. A note between the broker and buyer stating the exclusive-right-to-represent the buyer
 D. An agreement between the seller and buyer providing a grace period for backing out of the sale

82. _____ occurs when a tenant vacates a premise because the landlord failed to provide essential services.

 A. Quit notices
 B. Actual eviction
 C. Constructive eviction
 D. Notice to quit

83. A buyer has _____ to cancel a contract if a Seller's Disclosure Notice has not been provided prior to the effective date of the contract.?

 A. 9 days
 B. 7 days
 C. 30 days
 D. A Seller's Disclosure Notice is not necessary for buyers

84. Which is not true about the Federal Fair Housing Act?

 A. Prohibits discrimination in housing due to age
 B. Protects people from discrimination when renting or buying a home
 C. Prohibits refusal to sell or rent a house due to familial status
 D. All of the above

85. When a property loses value because of the lack of maintenance on natural wear and tear it is called _____.

    A. External depreciation
    B. Physical deterioration
    C. Economic obsolescence
    D. Negative amortization

86. Which of the following is an example of an appurtenance?

    A. Light bulbs
    B. Sofa
    C. Refrigerator
    D. Parking space

87. What is a syndicate?

    A. When one party operates a real estate investment
    B. When a party creates a real estate investment opportunity
    C. When two or more parties create and operate a real estate investment
    D. When a party builds a residential home for their family

88. Which of the following is a bundle of rights afforded to the buyer of real estate property?

    A. Right of control
    B. Right of exclusion
    C. Right of enjoyment
    D. All of the above

89. Which of the following is not a physical characteristic of land?

   A. Immobility
   B. Indestructability
   C. Square footage
   D. Uniqueness

90. A _____ is personal property that is used in a business and can be removed by the tenant when the lease ends.

   A. Escheat
   B. Trade fixtures
   C. Plottage
   D. Redlining

91. The _____ replaced dower and curtesy.

   A. Uniform Probate Code
   B. Real Estate Licensing Act
   C. Real Estate Code of Conduct
   D. Real Estate Code of Ethics

92. What is the highest possible ownership that can be held in real estate called?

   A. Fee simple absolute
   B. Estate at sufferance
   C. Defeasible
   D. Estate at will

93. Which of the following is an example of an encumbrance?

   A. Student loans
   B. Deed restriction
   C. Mortgage
   D. All of the above

94. The _____ determines the water usage in states where the water is scarce.

   A. Property rights
   B. Riparian rights
   C. Doctrine Appropriation
   D. Littoral rights

95. Which of the following is an example of a prescriptive easement?

   A. Building a fence on a neighbor's property
   B. Using a part of a neighbor's property to access the side of a road
   C. A neighbor uses another neighbor's Wi-Fi
   D. All of the above

96. A _____ is an interest in real property that is limited to the duration of the lifetime of the owner?

   A. Life estate
   B. Appurtenant easement
   C. Deed restriction
   D. Lien

97. This organization buys, owns and operates real estate for investors.

    A. National Investment Trust
    B. The Real Estate Investment Association
    C. Fair Housing Association
    D. Real Estate Investment Trust

98. Which tax is based on the value of real and personal property?

    A. Ad valorem tax
    B. Property tax
    C. Real estate tax
    D. Investment property tax

99. A _____ is a fixed object that is used as a permanent reference point to mark landownership boundaries.

    A. Datum
    B. Monument
    C. Metes and bounds
    D. Nonhomogeneity

100. What is a chain or title?

    A. A history of ownership regarding a property's title
    B. A line from which elevations are measured
    C. A comparison of homes sold in the same area
    D. The right a broker has to collect commission even if the property is not sold

THIS IS THE END OF THE NATIONAL PORTION.

State Portion

1. Which of the following is true about the GREC members?

   A. 5 of the 6 members must have a real estate license
   B. Must be a Georgia resident for a minimum of 5 years
   C. 1 member must have an interest in consumer affairs
   D. All of the above are true

2. Which of the following is an exception to commingling?

   A. When the buyer is a licensed agent
   B. Brokers may maintain enough personal funds in the account the meet the minimum balance required
   C. To pay off brokerage bills
   D. There is no exception

3. Which of the following is reason a broker can disburse trust funds?

   A. Upon rejection or withdrawal of offer
   B. At closing of contract
   C. With the written consent of all parties involved
   D. All of the above

4. Which of the following is true about trust accounts and property management?

   A. Rental payments must be made via electronic deposit
   B. Trust accounts cannot exceed $10,000
   C. Security deposits need to be held in an independent trust account
   D. All of the above are true

5. Georgia requires brokers to keep document from real estate transactions for _____ after the closing date.

   A. 5 years
   B. 3 years
   C. 10 years
   D. 6 months

6. Which of the following is true about real estate advertising in Georgia?

   A. Advertising costs cannot exceed 20% of revenue
   B. Each broker is required to put out advertisements a year
   C. No ad may be misleading or misrepresent any property
   D. All of the above is true

7. A licensee is legally required to _____.

   A. Present all written communications from one party to another during negotiations
   B. Give parties a copy of every signed document
   C. Advise parties on the best deal for the licensee
   D. A&B only

8. If a licensee is acting as a principal in a transaction the licensee must _____.

   A. Hire a broker
   B. Disclose that they are licensed
   C. Not act as the principal
   D. Designate another person to act as a principal

9. Before an offer is made, a licensee must _____ in writing to all parties.

   A. State who the licensee is working for
   B. Disclose the number of houses the licensee has worked for the specific party
   C. State the licensee's intention
   D. None of the above

10. Georgia prohibits _____ but may not apply when a licensee advertises their own property for sale.

   A. Blind ads
   B. Commercial advertisements
   C. Billboard advertisements
   D. None of the above

11. Which of the following documents is a broker not required to keep?

   A. Listing agreement
   B. Client lists
   C. Buyer agency agreement
   D. Purchase agreement

12. Georgia requires all brokers to maintain an accounting system that includes which of the following for each deposit into a trust fund.

   A. Name of parties
   B. Amount of deposit
   C. Date of deposit
   D. All of the above are required

13. Which of the following is not a category the GREC authority involves itself in?

A. Issuing licenses
B. Amending laws
C. Passing rules and regulations
D. All of the above are true

14. A _____ is where real estate borrowers apply for a loan.

A. A broker's office
B. The APR
C. Primary mortgage market
D. Savings and loan association

15. Which of the following is not a reason for disciplinary action by the GREC?

A. Failure to sell a home within 180 days
B. Acquiring a license by fraud or misrepresentation
C. Acting as a dual agent without consent
D. Paying commission to an unlicensed person

16. A _____ is legal in the state of Georgia and allows both parties to agree to have one agent or broker represent them.

A. General agency
B. Dual agency
C. Subagency
D. Special agency

17. Which of the following is an example of industrial real estate?

    A. New construction home
    B. Shopping center
    C. Warehouse
    D. Farm

18. In Georgia, a licensee that has been charged with a serious infraction is _____.

    A. Entitled to a hearing
    B. Required to surrender their license
    C. Required to pay a fine
    D. All of the above

19. What is the Georgia Homestead Exemption amount?

    A. $22,000
    B. $21,500
    C. $20,500
    D. $21,000

20. What are capital gains?

    A. The difference between the sale price of property and appraisal of property
    B. When a person sells land for more than they paid for it
    C. The excess cash given to a licensee for selling a home
    D. None of the above

21. A medical and education building is considered _____.

   A. Residential real estate
   B. Industrial real estate
   C. Commercial real estate
   D. Non-profit real estate

22. Which of the following is a disciplinary action the GREC can impose?

   A. Mandate a specific education program
   B. Suspend a license for a specified period of time
   C. Permanently revoke a license
   D. All of the above

23. Which of the following is not considered an improvement to a home in determining its cost basis?

   A. Converting to central heating and air
   B. Building a new fence
   C. Repairs to a leaky roof
   D. Repairs during a remodeling project

24. Georgia requires a _____ to conduct the closing on a real estate transaction.

   A. Licensed agent
   B. Broker
   C. Member of the commission
   D. Licensed attorney

25. Georgia requires a licensee to notify the GREC regarding any legal action against the licensee after the final disposition of any court or administrative case within _____.

    A. 10 days
    B. 24 hours
    C. 30 days
    D. 60 days

26. The Georgia Real Estate Recovery Fund will pay up to _____ for losses in a single transaction.

    A. $15,000
    B. $45,000
    C. $30,000
    D. $20,000

27. This federal antitrust law prohibits any agreement that has the effect of restraining trade.

    A. Conspiracy Act
    B. Sherman Act
    C. Federal Trade Commission Act
    D. None of the above

28. The Georgia Real Estate Education, Research and Recovery Fund must always maintain a minimum balance of _____.

    A. $100,000
    B. $1,000,000
    C. $500,000
    D. $750,000

29. This law, now recognized by most states, including Georgia, bans false advertising.

  A. Uniform Deceptive Trade Practices Act
  B. Sherman Act
  C. Clayton Act
  D. Fair Business Practice Act

30. If a licensee fails to pay damages to the injured party, the injured party may _____.

  A. May file for suspension of an agent or broker's license
  B. May take possession of a licensee's personal property with the approval of the court
  C. May provide written notice to the GREC for payment from the Recovery fund
  D. All of the above

31. What is the purpose of the Georgia Real Estate Education, Research and Recovery Fund?

  A. To protect the public against the illegal practices of brokers
  B. To provide education regarding real estate to the public
  C. To provide education and development for licensees
  D. A&C only

32. A licensee's license can be revoked for which of the follow?

  A. If the Georgia Real Estate Recovery Fund pays for losses caused by a licensee
  B. For failing to sell a home
  C. Failing to pass the license examination
  D. All of the above

33. A county or city cannot require a real estate brokerage or licensee to _____ unless that brokerage maintains a physical office within the county or city's jurisdiction.

    A. Pay a fixed-amount tax
    B. Be licensed within the state
    C. Receive commission
    D. Pay a gross receipts tax on commission earned

34. This Georgia antitrust law prohibits unfair and deceptive practices in the marketplace.

    A. Conspiracy Act
    B. Fair Business Practices Act
    C. Sherman Act
    D. Clayton Act

35. A _____ is an agreement to sell one property if the buyer purchases another property.

    A. Guaranteed sales plan
    B. Group boycott
    C. Tie-in arrangement
    D. Price fixing

36. A lease for years is not terminated by _____.

    A. The death of the party
    B. Constructive eviction
    C. Mutual agreement
    D. Actual eviction

37. Which of the following is not a standard approach to the appraisal of real property?

    A. Assessment approach
    B. Income approach
    C. Cost approach
    D. Market approach

38. _____ give owners an interest that extends to the center of the waterway.

    A. Littoral rights
    B. Riparian rights
    C. Correlative rights
    D. Prior appropriation

39. Acquiring absolute ownership to oil that naturally has funneled from a neighboring property onto yours is called _____.

    A. Rule of capture
    B. Littoral rights
    C. Fructus Industriales
    D. None of the above

40. A display counter placed in a leased commercial property is an example of _____.

    A. Accession
    B. Trade fixture
    C. Personal property
    D. Possessory estate

41. A display counter placed in a leased commercial property is an example of _____.

    A. Evaluate and vote on regulatory and procedural issues
    B. Devote 2-3 days a month to the commission
    C. Protect the public from harmful activities by people acting as real estate agents
    D. All of the above

42. The authority of the GREC is based upon _____.

    A. Common law
    B. Statutory law
    C. Corporate law
    D. Civil law

43. _____ is a water right that is on a first come, first serve basis.

    A. Littoral rights
    B. Riparian rights
    C. Correlative rights
    D. Prior appropriation

44. The GREC is required to do which of the follow in order to actively communicate with licensees and the public?

    A. Inform licensees and the public of actions taken by the commission and changes in laws
    B. Send out a weekly newsletter to all of the licensed agents
    C. Provide opportunities of discussion through regularly held forums
    D. A&C only

45. Georgia is a _____ state, which is something between a tax lien and a tax deed.

    A. Redeemable tax deed
    B. Judgement lien
    C. Property lien
    D. Decedent debt lien

46. This type of easement runs with the land and has two parties, one dominant and one servient.

    A. Private easement
    B. Easement in gross
    C. Appurtenance easement
    D. Utility easement

47. Recognized by the state of Georgia, _____ is when the interest of a deceased owner automatically transfers over to the remaining surviving owners.

    A. Tenancy by the entirety
    B. Joint tenancy with right of survivorship
    C. Tenancy in common
    D. Co-ownership

48. Which Georgia state law allows the buyer 7 days right of rescission for the purchase of a new condominium?

    A. Georgia Condominium Act
    B. Georgia Timeshare Law
    C. Condominium Act of Georgia
    D. There is no such law

49. Who has the right to exercise the power of eminent domain?

   A.   State government
   B.   Local government
   C.   Quasi-government groups
   D.   All of the above

50. Which of the following is true about Georgia eminent domain laws?

   A.   Landowners have the right to challenge eminent domain
   B.   The entity exercising the power of eminent domain must notify landowners prior to filing a petition
   C.   The entity exercising the power of eminent domain can use the property however they like
   D.   A&B only

51. This state law was created to regulate time-share programs.

   A.   Timeshare Act of Georgia
   B.   Georgia Time Share Act
   C.   Georgia Rental Property Act
   D.   There is no such law

52. Correlative rights allow an owner _____.

   A.   Full rights to a river or stream running through their property
   B.   Rights to a lake or pond adjacent to the property, in a public lot
   C.   A reasonable share of a common source of groundwater
   D.   A share of a body of water in a public area

THIS IS THE END OF THE STATE PORTION.

Answer Key – National Portion

1.	C	21.	D	41.	B	61.	D	81.	A
2.	A	22.	A	42.	A	62.	B	82.	C
3.	D	23.	C	43.	A	63.	D	83.	B
4.	A	24.	D	44.	C	64.	C	84.	A
5.	C	25.	D	45.	D	65.	A	85.	B
6.	B	26.	A	46.	A	66.	A	86.	D
7.	D	27.	A	47.	D	67.	A	87.	C
8.	C	28.	A	48.	A	68.	A	88.	D
9.	C	29.	B	49.	C	69.	C	89.	C
10.	A	30.	A	50.	D	70.	A	90.	B
11.	C	31.	B	51.	A	71.	C	91.	A
12.	C	32.	A	52.	B	72.	B	92.	A
13.	A	33.	B	53.	B	73.	A	93.	B
14.	A	34.	B	54.	B	74.	B	94.	C
15.	A	35.	A	55.	C	75.	B	95.	B
16.	B	36.	B	56.	A	76.	A	96.	A
17.	B	37.	B	57.	B	77.	B	97.	D
18.	C	38.	C	58.	A	78.	D	98.	A
19.	C	39.	C	59.	D	79.	C	99.	B
20.	A	40.	B	60.	C	80.	A	100.	A

1. **C) Foreclosure**

This is the legal process where a lender seeks to recover the balance of a loan by selling the property held as collateral. Foreclosure usually occurs after a lender has legally obtained a termination of the borrower's right of redemption.

2. **A) Asbestos**

Asbestos is a naturally occurring mineral and its insulation qualities make it popular in making fireproof materials. When products containing asbestos are disturbed, they release tiny fibers in the air that when inhaled over a long period of time can be detrimental as they accumulate in the lung causing scarring and inflammation. Continued exposure affects cells resulting in a rare cancer known as mesothelioma.

3. **D) Studs**

These are vertical beams that are used during construction to frame the house. They are used to form or position walls in a building. Previously, studs made of timber dominated the construction industry but modern construction styles have embraced the use of steel.

4. **A) Misrepresentation**

Misrepresentation occurs when a broker misstates information of property. It is a false statement that may affect a person's decision to enter into a contract. Three types of misrepresentation are fraudulent misrepresentation, negligent misrepresentation and innocent misrepresentation.

5. **C) Preventive maintenance**

In order to maintain tenants and an acceptable return on an investment, routine checks and repairs have to be done. These are done to safeguard against failing which may incur losses to the property manager that arise due to cost of replacement.

6. **B) Mortgagee**

A mortgagee is an entity that lends money for the purpose of buying a real estate property. As a precaution, the mortgagee establishes prior interest in the property and maintains the title as collateral.

7. **D) $156,250**

$150,000 / (1 - 0.04) = $156,250

8. **C) Land zoning**

This refers to the restriction of physical development and the use of certain parcels of land. It is done with regard to zoning laws and purposes to protect wildlife and natural resources. It is also used to restrict the number of domestic animals that can be accommodated on a property.

9. **C) Initiate judicial foreclosure**

Judicial foreclosure are court proceedings that allow the lender to seize the property that was held as collateral for sale. This is done in order to regain the principal amount. This can only be done once it has been established that a defaulting borrower is unable to continue making payments.

10. **A) American Land Title Association**

This is a trade association that is aimed at trying to improve oversight by representing title insurance.

11. **C) Fair Credit Reporting Act**

Credit reporting is the process of collecting and analyzing consumers credit information by credit bureaus. This information is sold to lending facilities in order to help them determine whether or not a borrower is eligible for a loan. This act was passed to highlight consumer rights when it comes to credit information.

12. **C) Right of egress**

This is the legal right granted to homeowners as they allow access to property. These rights are usually obtained through an easement and apply regardless of the property type.

13. **A) Sweat equity**

This is the non-monetary equity that owners contribute into the business or property. In this case, sweat equity is the amount of effort an owner puts into a property in order to increase its value.

14. **A) Buydown**

This is a mortgage-financing technique that allows a borrower to negotiate lower monthly payment rates. It usually involves the seller making payments to the lending institution to reduce monthly payment rate of the buyer. As a result, the purchase price goes up.

15. **A) Clear title**

A clear title is a title that has no liens or levies from creditors and other involved parties. A clear title is used to ensure there is no question of ownership. It shows that there are no outstanding financial responsibilities attached to the property and the owner is legally capable of selling the property.

16. **B) Credit report**

A credit report is a detailed breakdown of an individual's credit history and is usually carried out by credit bureaus. They use financial information attached to an individual like their bill payment to establish a unique report. This information is usually used by lenders while considering a loan applicant.

17. **B) Equity**

Equity is another term for ownership. In home investments, equity means the amount of principal that has been paid off. The higher the equity the easier it is to refinance a property.

18. **C) Notice of default**

This is a public notice filed in court regarding a borrower's default on a loan. It is usually to notify the borrower that there has been a breach in the contractual limit that had been predetermined in the loan. A grace period is included for negotiation before further action is considered.

19. **C) Lock-in period**

This is the period usually 30 to 60 days within which a lender is required to keep a loan offer open. This gives the borrower enough time to prepare for closing while the lender is processing the loan. A lock in period protects the borrower from losses incurred throughout the repayment of the loan caused by rising interest rates during processing of the loan.

20. **A) When a tenant breaks a rent prior to the date of expiry without a legal reason**

As a lease is a contract, breaking a lease without a valid reason may result in being sued by the landlord. To avoid legal action, the individual breaking the lease must prove beyond reasonable doubt that the break was caused by a situation completely out of their hands.

21. **D) Shortfall**

Shortfall is a term used to describe a situation where a financial obligation exceeds the required amount of cash available. A shortfall may be a temporary and current situation or a prolonged one. The latter represents mismanagement of funds and warrants a deeper look into spending habits and change has to be implemented.

22. **A) Tax abatement**

Tax abatement is a strategy used by the government to increase investments in specific areas. In the real estate sector, tax abatement occurs when taxes on properties are significantly reduced or completely eliminated. It is usually done to encourage investors to buy property in areas that have recorded long term low demand.

23. **C) $546,000**

$500,000 * 1.04 * 1.05 = $546,000

24. **D) Department of Health**

25. **D) $368,000**

$92,000 / 0.25 = $368,000

26.   **A) Abstract of title**

This is a summarized history of all title transfers and legal actions that have been connected with a certain property. It is beneficial in preventing home buyers from getting tangled in legal issues that are attached to a property. This is because any loss made because of a court ruling on a property once a buyer has purchased will be incurred by the new tenant.

27.   **A) Flashing**

This is a material used to cover joints where two or more types of material join. This usually happens to prevent water leakage through the joint. It also provides a drainage between two joints.

28.   **A) Eaves**

This is a part of the roof that projects over the wall beyond the edge of the roof. It is usually set in place to channel water away from the roof.

29.   **B) Cash on cash return**

Cash on cash return that a proven metric used to calculate future cash returns on a cash investment. This metric is only true for a cash investment and does not take into account loan investments.

30.   **A) Architectural Review Board**

The Architectural Review Board is given the responsibility of upholding the visual integrity of a town. It is responsible for reviewing all exterior designs of all residential and commercial structures in a town. All new structures and structures that are up for alteration are required to provide a blueprint of the exterior design for printing. They are also charged with ensuring commercial signs conform to the towns design.

31.   **B) Gross lease**

A gross lease is a lease where a flat rent fee is paid. It includes rent and other utility fees such as taxes and insurance. A landlord is obligated to calculate a rate based on history or research. A negotiation between the tenant and landlord can also be reached on the services the tenant wants to be included in the lease.

32.   **A) House rules**

These are rules that are given to tenants of a coop or condo on the beginning of the contract regarding behavior within the complex. They are put in place to ensure a comfortable living space for all occupants. Failure to adhere to the rules may result in eviction.

33.   **B) Absorption rate**

This is a ration of the number of properties that have been sold against the number of properties that are available for sale within a specified area.

34.   **B) Acceleration clause**

This is a provision in a mortgage that allows the lender the right to demand the immediate settlement on a mortgage under certain predetermined conditions such as a borrower defaulting on a loan.

35.   **A) Easement appurtenant**

Easement appurtenant is an agreement that is transferable with ownership rights of a property. When a property is transferred through sale or inheritance, all rights and privileges attached to the land are automatically transferred to the new owner.

36.   **B) Homeowner's warranty insurance**

Homeowner's warranty insurance insures the homeowner from the builder's faults for a specified warranty period

37.   **B) Adverse possession**

This is a legal principle that allows a person who has been living on a specific land for a long period of time to take possession of the land without permission of the owner. The individual does not have to have a title to the land to acquire it. The title holder is capable of claiming his land by choosing to eject the squatter.

38.   **C) Encumbrance**

This is a limitation against a real estate property. It restricts the owner from transferring ownership of the title. It also prevents an owner from depreciating the value of the property.

39.   **C) Joists**

These are horizontal structural members used to frame an open space. They are often used in transferring loads to the vertical members of the structure. When used in floors, they provide stiffness in the framing systems.

40.   **B) Conveyance**

A conveyance or sale deed is a legally binding contract that transfers all ownership rights from the seller to the buyer. It usually states the agreed-on price, the date of the transaction and the obligations of the parties involved.

41.   **B) Non-solicitation order**

This is an order issued to broker and agents to prevent them from soliciting listings in designated areas

42.   **A) Colleges**

Despite the fact that all property is assessed to determine its value, universities, schools, parks, government institutions, religious organizations, and hospitals are exempt from property taxes. Veterans are also eligible from partial exemption from taxes.

43.   **A) Accountability**

Commingling is a contract breach where a fiduciary mixed funds belonging to a client with his own making it impossible to separate them. The accountability clause requires a fiduciary to be able to maintain an accurate report of documents and funds that he/she has been entrusted.

44.   **C) Eminent domain**

This is the government's power to take private land for public use under certain circumstances. It is defined by the Taking Clause of the Fifth Amendment which prohibits the taking of private land without just compensation. It emphasizes that the government can only take land for public use and offer just compensation on the land.

45.   **D) Refuse modifications for handicapped tenants**

Refuse to allow tenants to make reasonable structural modifications to a unit at the tenant's expense to allow the handicapped tenant full enjoyment of the property (Fair Housing Act). In accordance with the Fair Housing Act which is against discrimination in housing, multifamily buildings are expected to ensure accessibility for people using wheelchairs

46.   **A) The Americans with Disabilities Act of 1990**

This act was enacted to ensure disabled people are not discriminated against and have equal rights regarding access to employment and commercial facilities.

47.   **D) Tenancy at will**

This is a tenancy that is not bound by a lease and does not have an expiry or duration of tenancy. A predetermined payment plan is adhered and a tenant is flexible to terminate the tenancy without legal proceedings. It is a beneficial plan for landlords and tenants that seek flexibility.

48.   **A) $2,041**

($350,000 * 0.07) / 12 = $2,041

49. **C) Civil Rights Act Amendment of 1974**

The Civil Rights act amendment of 1974 banned discrimination based on sex and credit in a congress proceeding. Women being offered maternity leave on the assumption that they were unable to work was rendered illegal and sexist teaching methods were discredited.

50. **D) Handicaps and familial status**

The act protects people with disabilities and families with children. Pregnant women were also protected from illegal discrimination.

51. **A) $70,000**

$500,000 * 0.14 = $70,000

52. **B) Assessor**

An assessor is a government official that is engaged to determine the value of a property. The information gathered by an assessor is used to calculate future property taxes. Assessors maintain annual assessments at a uniform percentage of market value.

53. **B) Amortization**

This is the scheduling of monthly mortgage payments showing breakdown of payment. When paying a mortgage loan for a property, the initial payments are put towards paying off the interest and less is allocated to the principal amount. As a borrower makes more payments, more is allocated to the principal and less to the interest.

54. **B) Real estate tax**

This is an ad valorem tax on the value of a property. It is levied annually on real estate by the government authority.

55. **C) Leverage**

This refers to money that has been borrowed to finance an investment property. The leverage concept works best when rent and property values are on the rise. Monthly mortgage payments for the rental property become constant which results in a rise in profits

56. **A) Forced air system**

A forced air system refers to any HVAC system that makes use of air ducts and vents to release temperature-controlled air into the building. A forced air system released filtered and dehumidified cold air into buildings and runs at an affordable price. A central air system on the other hand uses vents in the forced air system to provide cool and conditioned air.

57. **B) One year**

An individual is required to wait for an entire year after which the agent is required to prove with evidence that he/she is capable of being trustworthy and upholding the law with regard to the real estate sector.

58. **A) Board of directors**

A co-op is an alternative method to traditional housing. A board of directors is elected by the shareholders to run the corporation. They are responsible for vetting and doing background checks on potential new shareholders in the corporation. They are also responsible for upholding the values and regulations of the co-op and terminating tenancy of individuals found to be acting contrary to the rules.

59. **D) Abstraction method**

This is a method of estimating the value of a piece of land that is based on the going price of similar parcels of land within the area.

60. **C) Grantor**

This is the party that transfers ownership of property to buyer through a legal document known as a deed. The grantor is required to sign the deed admitting the transfer of ownership before closing. The deed is then filed at the county jurisdiction for public record.

61. **D) Radon**

Radon is a radioactive cancer-causing gas that comes from the natural breakdown of uranium in soil. The gas penetrates its way into houses from cracks and holes in the foundation. Testing for radon gas is mandatory during purchasing of a home in order to fix the problem by lowering the amount of radon gas available to the acceptable amounts.

62. **B) Riparian rights**

These are rights that arise when an individual owns land near a moving watercourse. These rights include swimming and irrigation. The rights only attach when there's a water on one side of the land. An individual is allowed to benefit from the water body without contaminating or altering the flow of the waterbody.

63. **D) Regulation Z**

It requires lenders to make comprehensive disclosure statements to borrowers for consumer loans. It is aimed at protecting consumers from misleading lending practices. Lenders are required to disclose interest rates, finance charges, explain terms used and respond to all complaints launched by the borrower. This law was passed to ensure that borrowers make informed credit choices.

64.   **C) Right of first refusal**

This is the right given to a specific party to purchase or lease a property before it is open to bidding by other potential buyers. The party being offered the privilege is not obligated to buy the property. In the event that the party is not interested in the property, it is opened up to the public.

65.   **A) Economic obsolescence**

This is the decrease in the market value of a property due to external factors that cannot be controlled by the property owner i.e. building of an interstate highway close to a prime property. Its value immediately decreases due to the noise pollution.

66.   **A) Special agent**

A special agent is an agent whose services are only employed for a specific task. Once the task is completed a special agent no longer has authority to represent the client.

67.   **A) Appraisal**

An appraisal in a professional opinion value assessment of a property and is independent of the market values of similar properties based on the fact that all properties are unique and cannot be compared to each other.

68.   **A) Mechanic's lien**

This is a security interest in title of property for the benefit of those who supplied materials and offered professional services on the construction and renovation of a property. A mechanic's lien can be taken on both real and personal properties.

69.   **C) Sill plate**

This is a horizontal member of a wall where vertical members of the building are attached. It usually lies between the foundation and floor frame.

70.   **A) Phone**

This is because salespeople are considered independent contractors and therefore are not eligible for company benefits.

71.   **C) First substantial contact**

This refers to the earliest practicable opportunity during a conversation with the consumer. An agency disclosure is to be provided to disclose and explain the nature of the representation in a real estate transaction.

72.   **B) Guiding families with children into an apartment building with other families with children and away from other buildings**

Steering is an unlawful practice that violates the federal fair housing provisions. It is a practice in which brokers influence the choice of a prospective buyer or tenant.

73.   **A) 1% of loan**

A value point is a fee paid directly to the lender at closing in exchange for a reduced interest rate and can lower a borrower's monthly mortgage payment.

74.   **B) Independent contractors**

Independent contractors are hired to perform a service but are not included in the employee catalogue. Their main goal is to complete the task and the employing broker has no control over the process of yielding results or financial expenses incurred.

75.   **B) Accessory building**

This is a building that is built separately from the main structure in a property. It is usually put to use for a specific purpose such as a shed, workshop or garage.

76.   **A) Fee simple estate**

This provides absolute ownership of the land and allows the owner to do whatever they choose to with the land. This is the highest form of ownership in real estate.

77.   **B) Income that is earned by one spouse during the marriage**

Community property is defined as everything that a married couple owns together. This includes income and property acquired during the duration of the marriage.

78.   **D) Real property**

A fixture is physically property that is permanently attached to real property (on it or under it), that cannot be moved. Examples include ponds, canals, buildings and roads.

79.   **C) Mutual Agreement**

An agreement between a buyer and a seller. It is a binding contract between the two parties and includes any contingencies.

80.   **A) A listing agreement with the seller has been executed**

A listing agreement is a contract between the homeowner and a selling agent. It is a legal agreement that gives the selling agent the right to sell the home.

81. **A) An agreement between the mortgage company and borrower that shows the terms of the loan**

This binding note states the terms of the loan and that the borrower promises to for the loan. It also provides evidence of the loan and both parties must sign the note to make it legally binding.

82. **C) Constructive eviction**

A constructive eviction is when a tenant must move out because the landlord fails to do something which renders the property uninhabitable. The tenant needs to give notice of the condition and allow a reasonable amount of time for the landlord to fix it. If this does not occur, the tenant can move out.

83. **B) 7 days**

If a seller's disclosure notice is not provided to the buyer, then they buyer has 7 days to cancel the contract.

84. **A) Prohibits discrimination in housing due to age**

The Federal Fair Housing Law prohibits discrimination due to race, color, national origin, religion, sex, familiar status and disability. This act prohibits discrimination when renting or buying a home, getting a mortgage, seeking housing assistance or engaging in other housing-related activities.

85. **B) Physical deterioration**

This is the most obvious form of depreciation and can occur when maintenance does not keep up with natural wear and tear. It causes a loss of value to the property. There are two types of physical deterioration functional obsolescence and external obsolescence.

86. **D) Parking space**

Appurtenances are real property that is immovable or fixed to the land. Parking spaces and water rights are considered an appurtenance.

87. **C) When two or more parties create and operate a real estate investment**

A syndicate is when investors pool their financial and intellectual resources to invest in real estate properties. These investments are bigger than a party would be able to afford individually.

88. **D) All of the above**

The right of disposition is also a bundle of rights. It is a set of legal privileges that affords a real estate buyer when the transfer of title occurs.

89. **C) Square footage**

Land has three characteristics, immobility, indestructibility and uniqueness. Some of the characteristics are immovable and can be changed, but location is an immobile characteristic.

90. **B) Trade fixtures**

Trade fixtures are removable personal property that is attached by the tenant to a leased land for the purpose of business i.e. display county. The trade fixture must be removable without damage to the property.

91. **A) Uniform Probate Code**

The Uniform Probate Code states that when a spouse dies the surviving spouse can take an elective share on the death of their spouse. It is an act that was drafted by the National Conference of Commissioners on Uniform State Laws.

92. **A) Fee simple absolute**

The fee simple absolute is the maximum possible right of ownership in real property. It is a form of freehold ownership and continues forever.

93. **B) Deed restrictions**

An encumbrance is a limitation or liability against real estate. A lien, deed restriction, easements, encroachments and licenses are all encumbrances. It restricts the owner's ability to transfer the property title.

94. **C) Doctrine of Appropriation**

The Doctrine of Appropriation says that water rights are determined by priority of beneficial use. The first person to use water or divert the water for beneficial purposes can acquire the individual rights to the water.

95. **B) Using a part of a neighbor's property to access the side of a road**

Prescriptive easement is when the right to use another's land is acquired through continued use without permission. There are three different types of easement: easement in gross, easement appurtenant and prescriptive easement. Regulations differ from state to state.

96. **A) Life estate**

A life estate lasts the duration of a person's life. It is also called a life tenancy. The estate in real property ends at the death and ownership of the property reverts back to the original owner.

97. **D) Real Estate Investment Trust**

This company owns and operates income-producing real estate. REIT owns commercial property such as apartment buildings, warehouses, hospitals and shopping centers.

98. **A) Ad valorem tax**

The ad valorem tax is based on the value of the property. It is imposed at the time of a transaction just like a value-added tax.

99. **B) Monument**

A natural or manmade, fixed object that is used as a reference point for surveying land. It is a tangible landmark that has been established to indicate a boundary.

100. **A) A history of ownership regarding a property's title**

A chain of title goes back to the original owner of the property and is the sequence of historical transfers of title. A chain of title search typically goes back 40 years to ensure there are no defects.

Answer Key – State Portion

1.	D	21.	B	41.	D
2.	B	22.	D	42.	B
3.	D	23.	C	43.	D
4.	C	24.	D	44.	D
5.	B	25.	A	45.	A
6.	C	26.	A	46.	C
7.	D	27.	B	47.	B
8.	B	28.	B	48.	A
9.	A	29.	A	49.	D
10.	A	30.	C	50.	D
11.	B	31.	D	51.	B
12.	D	32.	A	52.	C
13.	B	33.	A		
14.	C	34.	B		
15.	A	35.	C		
16.	B	36.	A		
17.	C	37.	A		
18.	A	38.	B		
19.	B	39.	A		
20.	B	40.	B		

1. **D) All of the above are true**

    The licensed members must have been actively licensed for 5 years and the non-licensed member must not have any interest in the real estate industry.

2. **B) Brokers may maintain enough personal funds in the account the meet the minimum balance required**

    The other exception to commingling is that a broker can maintain enough personal funds in the account to pay a service charge or leave commission funds in trust account.

3. **D) All of the above**

    They can also be disbursed after reasonable interpretation of contract or as directed by a court order.

4. **C) Security deposits need to be held in an independent trust account**

    Property managers must keep security deposits, and rental payments & other operating funds in separate trust accounts in separate trust accounts.

5. **B) 3 years**

The documents must also be available for inspection and the commission has the ability to audit the records.

6. **C) No ad may be misleading or misrepresent any property**

False advertising is a violation of license laws and the advertising cannot be misleading or misrepresent property, sale terms, services, or policies.

7. **D) A&B only**

The licensee is required to present all written communication from one party to another and the licensee is required to give parties a copy of every document they sign.

8. **B) Disclose that they are licensed**

If a licensee is acting as a principal in a transaction, then they are required to disclose that they are licensed.

9. **A) State who the licensee is working for**

The licensee is required to disclose in writing who the licensee is working for and from whom the licensee will receive compensation, to all parties.

10. **A) Blind ad**

Blind ads are advertisements that fail to include the name of the broker and licensee or fails to state that the add was placed by a licensee. It is prohibited in Georgia and a licensee must have written permission to advertise their own property without the broker's name.

11. **B) Client lists**

Brokers are required to keep all documents from real estate transactions. Other documents required are lease or rental agreements, trust account records and closing statements.

12. **D) All of the above are required**

Identification of property involved, and the amount paid, and date of each check is also required. The accounting system can be either manual or electronic.

13. **B) Amending laws**

Amending laws is something that the GREC does not involves itself in, however they are able to pass rules and regulations. They can also impose disciplinary action and establish fees.

14.   **C) Primary mortgage market**

The primary mortgage market is also where a borrower receives a loan and makes loan payments to.

15.   **A) Failure to sell a home within 180 days**

Failure to sell a home cannot result in disciplinary action. Other reasons are failing to include an expiration date in a listing, demonstrating incompetence or dishonesty and accepting or giving undisclosed commissions.

16.   **B) Dual agency**

In this type of agency, neither party is exclusively represented by a designated real estate agent.

17.   **C) Warehouse**

A warehouse is a type of industrial real estate. Other types are manufacturing buildings or buildings used for research, storage, production, or distribution of goods.

18.   **A) Entitled to a hearing**

If a licensee has been charged with a serious infraction, then the licensee can have a hearing. The licensee must receive written notice of date, time, and location of hearing as well as the statement of charges.

19.   **B) $21,500**

The Georgia Homestead Exemption amount is $21,500 of the home or property that has been covered by the homestead exemption.

20.   **B) When a person sells land for more than they paid for it**

Capital gains is the excess money made from the sale of a property or land. This excess money is subject to taxes.

21.   **B) Commercial real estate**

Commercial real estate is hotels, offices, strip malls and even apartments buildings because they are owned to produce income.

22.   **D) All of the above**

The GREC can use all of the listed disciplinary actions. They can also require periodic reports due to an account violation, impose a fine, reprimand, and issue a citation.

23. **C) Repairs to a leaky roof**

A cost basis is a property's purchase price and acquisition expenses plus additional expenses. A repair to a home does not determine a cost basis but a fence, remodeling repairs and central health and air does.

24. **D) Licensed attorney**

Georgia requires a licensed attorney to conduct a closing in order for it to be legal.

25. **A) 10 days**

The GREC must be notified within 10 days. This is for cases that name the licensee and is related to a violation of license law.

26. **A) $15,000**

The Recovery fund will pay up to $15,000 for losses in a single transaction and $45,000 for losses caused by one licensee.

27. **B) Sherman Act**

The Sherman Act prohibits activities that restrict the interstate commerce and competition in the marketplace. This act was amended by the Clayton Act.

28. **B) $1,000,000**

The fund must have a minimum of one million dollars and if it falls below that, each licensee, at the time of renewal, may be required to pay 30 dollars for each year in the renewal period.

29. **A) Uniform Deceptive Trade Practices Act**

This act is recognized by most states and makes false advertising a misdemeanor charge. It also allows victims to sue for damages.

30. **C) May provide written notice to the GREC for payment from the Recovery fund**

The injured party, upon failure to recover payment from the licensee has the option of notifying the GREC and applying for payment from the recovery fund.

31. **D) A&C only**

This fund protects against illegal practices of brokers and provides education and development for licensees in the state. This fund was created and maintained by new licensees paying into the fund.

32. **A) If the Georgia Real Estate Recovery Fund pays for losses caused by a licensee**

A licensee will have their license revoked if the fund pays for losses on behalf of the licensee. The license can be reinstated once the money is returned to the fund with interest.

33. **A) Pay a fixed-amount tax**

The county or city is able to charge a gross receipts tax on brokers for commission earned within the jurisdiction.

34. **B) Fair Business Practices Act**

This state antitrust law prohibits unfair and deceptive acts of practice in the marketplace and applies to consumer transactions involving the sale, lease or rental of goods, services, and property for personal, family or household purposes.

35. **C) Tie-in arrangement**

In this type of agreement, a seller agrees to sell one piece of property only if the buyer agrees to buy another piece of property.

36. **A) The death of a party**

The death of a party does not terminate a lease. Constructive eviction, actual eviction and mutual agreement does terminate a lease.

37. **A) Assessment approach**

The three standard approaches to the appraisal of real property is income approach, cost approach and market approach.

38. **B) Riparian rights**

These rights give owners an interest which extends to the center of the waterway. It is the right to use water from a non-navigable stream or river.

39. **A) Rule of capture**

This law states that the first person to capture a natural resource owns that resource. The rule helps in determining the ownership of natural resources such as oil, groundwater, and gas,

40. **B) Trade fixture**

Trade fixtures are removable personal property that a tenant attaches to leased land for a business purpose. This must be removed at the end of a lease.

41. **D) All of the above**

The commissions duties include all of the above. Other duties include assuring licensees meet basic levels of competency and create a regulatory environment for the industry that is reasonable and allows the licensee to attain economic success.

42. **B) Statutory law**

Statutory law is typically enacted by a legislative body. It varies from regulatory or administrative law passed by executive agencies or common law.

43. **D) Prior appropriation**

Prior appropriation is first come first serve. The waters need to not be used on land abutting a stream or river.

44. **D) A&C only**

The commission is not required to send out weekly newsletters to licensed agents and brokers. They are required to inform licensees and the public about changes in laws and any actions the commission take. Also, they must provide opportunities of discussion between the public and licenses and the commission.

45. **A) Redeemable tax deed**

This means that at a redeemable tax deed sale, a person is purchasing the deed to property and the owner can redeem the property by paying for the deed at its bid prices plus interest or a penalty.

46. **C) Appurtenant easement**

This type of easement is a right to use adjoining property that transfers with the land. The dominant tenement benefits from the easement and the servient tenement provides the easement.

47. **B) Joint tenancy with right of survivorship**

This type of tenancy is a joint property ownership that affords co-owners the right to a share of the property upon the death of an owner.

48. **A) Georgia Condominium Act**

This law requires extensive disclosures and gives the buyer 7 days right of recission when buying a condominium from the developer.

49.   **D) All of the above**

Eminent domain can be exercised by the federal, state, and local government. Quasi-government groups, such as hospital and stadium authorities, also have the right to eminent domain.

50.   **D) A&B only**

Written notice prior to the petition and definition of public use as specifically for roads or government use must be stated. They must also give the landowners a copy of their rights. The landowner also has the right to challenge the eminent domain and challenge the compensation being offered.

51.   **B) Georgia Time Share Act**

This state law regulates the time-share programs in the state as well as out-of-state properties sold in state.

52.   **C) A reasonable share of a common source of groundwater**

Correlative rights provide an owner a reasonable share of water, but as long as the share does not adversely affect downstream neighbors.

Practice Test 3

Directions:

1. You have a 4-hour time limit to complete the whole exam.

2. To pass, aim to answer at least 75 out of 100 questions correctly on the national portion **AND** at least 39 out of 52 questions on the state portion.

3. Some questions will require mathematics. You may use a calculator.

4. **Phones and pagers are not allowed. Having either will result in automatic dismissal from the exam and nullification of exam scores.**

Tips:

- Answer all questions even if you are unsure.
- Mark any questions you are stuck on and revisit them after you are done. The exam is timed so make sure you finish as many questions as you can.
- After reading the question, try answering it in your head first to avoid getting confused by the choices.
- Read the entire question before looking at the answers.
- Use the process of elimination to filter out choices that don't seem correct to increase your chances of selecting the correct answer.
- Be aware of important keywords like **not, sometimes, always,** and **never**. These words completely alter the ask of the question so it's important to keep track of them.

PLEASE READ THESE INSTRUCTIONS CAREFULLY.

Name: Belinda

Practice Test 3

(27)

73/100

NATIONAL PORTION

Date: _____

1. Ⓐ Ⓐ Ⓑ ● Ⓓ
2. ● Ⓑ Ⓒ Ⓓ
3. Ⓐ Ⓑ ● Ⓓ
4. Ⓐ Ⓑ Ⓒ ●
5. Ⓐ Ⓑ Ⓒ ●
6. ● Ⓑ Ⓒ Ⓓ
7. B Ⓐ Ⓑ Ⓒ Ⓓ
8. Ⓐ Ⓑ ● Ⓓ
9. Ⓐ Ⓑ ● Ⓓ
10. B Ⓐ Ⓑ Ⓒ ●
11. ● Ⓑ Ⓒ Ⓓ
12. Ⓐ Ⓑ Ⓒ ●
13. Ⓐ Ⓑ Ⓒ ●
14. C Ⓐ Ⓑ Ⓒ ●
15. Ⓐ Ⓑ Ⓒ ●
16. Ⓐ ● Ⓒ Ⓓ
17. Ⓐ Ⓑ ● Ⓓ
18. B Ⓐ Ⓑ ● Ⓓ
19. Ⓐ Ⓑ Ⓒ ●
20. A ● Ⓑ Ⓒ Ⓓ
21. C Ⓐ Ⓑ Ⓒ ●
22. A Ⓐ Ⓑ ● Ⓓ
23. Ⓐ Ⓑ ● Ⓓ
24. Ⓐ Ⓑ ● Ⓓ
25. Ⓐ ● Ⓒ Ⓓ
26. A Ⓐ ● Ⓒ Ⓓ
27. Ⓐ ● Ⓒ Ⓓ
28. C Ⓐ ● Ⓒ Ⓓ
29. Ⓐ Ⓑ ● Ⓓ
30. A ● Ⓑ Ⓒ Ⓓ

31. B Ⓐ Ⓑ Ⓒ Ⓓ
32. D Ⓐ Ⓑ Ⓒ Ⓓ
33. Ⓐ Ⓑ Ⓒ Ⓓ
34. Ⓐ Ⓑ Ⓒ Ⓓ
35. Ⓐ Ⓑ ● Ⓓ
36. Ⓐ Ⓑ Ⓒ Ⓓ
37. A Ⓐ Ⓑ ● Ⓓ
38. Ⓐ Ⓑ Ⓒ ●
39. A Ⓐ Ⓑ Ⓒ Ⓓ
40. Ⓐ Ⓑ Ⓒ Ⓓ
41. Ⓐ Ⓑ Ⓒ Ⓓ
42. Ⓐ Ⓑ ● Ⓓ
43. Ⓐ ● Ⓒ Ⓓ
44. D Ⓐ Ⓑ Ⓒ Ⓓ
45. Ⓐ ● Ⓒ Ⓓ
46. Ⓐ Ⓑ ● Ⓓ
47. B Ⓐ Ⓑ Ⓒ ●
48. Ⓐ Ⓑ Ⓒ ●
49. ● Ⓑ Ⓒ Ⓓ
50. ● Ⓑ Ⓒ Ⓓ
51. Ⓐ Ⓑ ● Ⓓ
52. ● Ⓑ Ⓒ Ⓓ
53. ● Ⓑ Ⓒ Ⓓ
54. Ⓐ Ⓑ Ⓒ ●
55. ● Ⓑ Ⓒ Ⓓ
56. ● Ⓑ Ⓒ Ⓓ
57. Ⓐ Ⓑ Ⓒ Ⓓ
58. ● Ⓑ Ⓒ Ⓓ
59. Ⓐ ● Ⓒ Ⓓ
60. ● Ⓑ Ⓒ Ⓓ

61. ● Ⓑ Ⓒ Ⓓ
62. B Ⓐ Ⓑ Ⓒ ●
63. ● Ⓑ Ⓒ Ⓓ
64. D Ⓐ Ⓑ ● Ⓓ
65. Ⓐ ● Ⓒ Ⓓ
66. ● Ⓑ Ⓒ Ⓓ
67. Ⓐ ● Ⓒ Ⓓ
68. Ⓐ Ⓑ ● Ⓓ
69. D Ⓐ Ⓑ Ⓒ Ⓓ
70. A Ⓐ ● Ⓒ Ⓓ
71. ● Ⓑ Ⓒ Ⓓ
72. D Ⓐ Ⓑ Ⓒ Ⓓ
73. Ⓐ Ⓑ ● Ⓓ
74. Ⓐ ● Ⓒ Ⓓ
75. Ⓐ Ⓑ Ⓒ ●
76. Ⓐ Ⓑ ● Ⓓ
77. Ⓐ Ⓑ Ⓒ ●
78. ● Ⓑ Ⓒ Ⓓ
79. D Ⓐ Ⓑ ● Ⓓ
80. Ⓐ ● Ⓒ Ⓓ
81. Ⓐ Ⓑ Ⓒ ●
82. ● Ⓑ Ⓒ Ⓓ
83. Ⓐ Ⓑ ● Ⓓ
84. Ⓐ ● Ⓒ Ⓓ
85. Ⓐ ● Ⓒ Ⓓ
86. A Ⓐ Ⓑ ● Ⓓ
87. Ⓐ Ⓑ ● Ⓓ
88. Ⓐ ● Ⓒ Ⓓ
89. ● Ⓑ Ⓒ Ⓓ
90. Ⓐ Ⓑ Ⓒ ●

91. B Ⓐ Ⓑ Ⓒ ●
92. ● Ⓑ Ⓒ Ⓓ
93. Ⓐ Ⓑ ● Ⓓ
94. Ⓐ ● Ⓒ Ⓓ
95. Ⓐ Ⓑ ● Ⓓ
96. Ⓐ Ⓑ ● Ⓓ
97. Ⓐ Ⓑ ● Ⓓ
98. Ⓐ ● Ⓒ Ⓓ
99. ● Ⓑ Ⓒ Ⓓ
100. Ⓐ Ⓑ Ⓒ ●

National Portion

1. What is the name given to the estimate amount on a mortgage?

    A. Pre-approval
    B. Post-approval
    C. Principal
    D. Mortgage

2. What is the actual amount of space a tenant can lay carpet and place furniture?

    A. Usable Square Footage
    B. Rentable square footage
    C. Common areas
    D. Service areas

3. What is the name given to an amount of money borrowed to facilitate the purchase of a property?

    A. Escrow
    B. Interest
    C. Down payment
    D. Principal

4. What type of mortgage loan is made available through the United States Department of Veterans Affairs?

    A. Blanket mortgage
    B. Balloon mortgage
    C. Graduated mortgage
    D. VA mortgage

5. What is the value obtained by deducting applied payments from original amortization?

    A. Full term
    B. Paid term
    C. Principal term
    D. Remaining term

6. What is the arrangement that allows a seller to lease a property from a purchaser after selling it?

    A. Leaseback
    B. Leasehold
    C. Sublease
    D. Proprietary lease

7. What type of easement attaches rights to a tenant instead of the land?

    A. Easement appurtenant
    B. Easement in gross
    C. Prescriptive easement
    D. All the above

8. What is the penalty charge for paying back a loan ahead of the scheduled payment plan?

    A. Defaulting penalty
    B. Interest
    C. Prepayment penalty
    D. Principal amount

9. What is an insurance premium paid by the buyer to the lender in order to protect the lender from default on a mortgage?

   A. Hazard insurance
   B. Homeowner's insurance
   C. Private mortgage insurance
   D. Title insurance

10. What is the name given to a party that acts in conjunction with a lender to originate a loan?

    A. Mortgage broker
    B. Third party originator
    C. Lender
    D. Intermediate

11. What is the term used to describe the alteration of a property in order to increase its market value?

    A. Capital Improvement
    B. Preventive maintenance
    C. Appreciation
    D. Common charges

12. What is the tax levied on transfer of property?

    A. Capital gains tax
    B. Deductible tax
    C. Property tax
    D. Transfer tax

13. Which of the following is an appraisal method in real estate?

    A. Sales Comparison Approach
    B. Cost Approach
    C. Income Approach
    D. All of the above

14. For at least how long must an asset be held before being sold to be categorized as long-term capital gains?

    A. One month
    B. Six months
    C. One year
    D. Two years

15. Which of these is considered an operating expense?

    A. Repairs
    B. Depreciation
    C. Payroll
    D. All of the above

16. What is an unlawful detainer?

    A. Forcing rent payments for tenants who have already moved out
    B. Refusing to leave a property despite expiration or termination of lease
    C. Listing a property whose lease has not expired
    D. Subletting a property without permission from the landlord

17. What is the freeze placed on a mortgage loan for a period of time?

   A. Cessation
   B. Amortization
   C. Rate lock
   D. Interest freeze

18. What type of lease gives the tenant an option to purchase the property?

   A. Leaseback
   B. Lease option
   C. Leasehold
   D. Gross lease

19. What is conditioner capacity?

   A. This is the capacity of an air conditioner to heat or cool the room
   B. The space used up by an air conditioner
   C. The strength of an air conditioner
   D. The cooling capacity of an air conditioner and is measured in tons

20. What is the name given to an individual that acts in intermediate for brokers and lenders?

   A. Mortgage broker
   B. Mortgage banker
   C. Attorney
   D. Intermediate

21. If a property is taxed at 30% with a tax levy of $105,000, what is its assessed value?

   A. $136,500
   B. $146,666
   C. $350,000
   D. None of the above

   105,000 / .3

22. What is the notice given when a tenant has a pet in a complex that has no pets policy?

   A. Notice to cure
   B. Notice to quit
   C. Notice of default
   D. Notice of termination

23. What is a roof's vertical rise in inches divided by its horizontal span in feet?

   A. Depth
   B. Width
   C. Pitch
   D. Length

24. Who engages the services of a broker?

   A. The client
   B. The neighbor
   C. The contractor
   D. The appraiser

25. Right of way would be best defined as?

A. Escheat
B. Easement
C. Right of ingress
D. Encumbrance

26. Who can get partial exemptions from property taxes?

A. Disabled
B. Schools
C. Shelters
D. Markets

27. What age must a person be to get a Real Estate license?

A. 16 years
B. 18 years
C. 30 years
D. 43 years

28. Which electricity conductor plays the same role as a circuit board?

A. Cell
B. Capacitor
C. Fuse
D. Switch

29. What is the definition of a bilateral contract?

A. A contract that involves only the promisor
B. A contract that involves only the promisee
C. A contract that involves both a promisor and promisee
D. A contract that allows both parties to drop all claims and get out of the contract

30. What is real property tax based on?

A. Assessed value
B. CMA
C. Appraisal
D. Taxable value

31. What agency is responsible for protecting wetlands?

A. CERCLA
B. Environmental Protection Agency
C. FEMA
D. NY Health Department

32. What is a schedule of the projected future income and expenses for a real estate investment?

A. IOU
B. Invoice
C. Promissory note
D. Pro Forma Statement

33. What is an agent required to do if a client refuses to sign an agency disclosure form?

    A. Terminate relationship
    B. Create record of refusal in writing
    C. Continue without record of the refusal
    D. Take legal action against the client

34. What is a general voluntary lien?

    A. Mortgage
    B. Taxes
    C. Revenues
    D. Duties

35. If a salesperson's commission is not paid, he resorts to?

    A. Buyer
    B. Seller
    C. Broker
    D. Lender

36. What type of tenancy exists where property is owned by a single individual?

    A. Joint tenancy
    B. Ownership in severalty
    C. Tenancy in entirety
    D. Tenancy in common

37. Who are testers in real estate?

    A. People who pose as real estate clients to check if fair housing is being practiced
    B. People who assess the value of a property
    C. People who pose as borrowers to ensure proper loaning practices
    D. People who approach the seller without the intention of buying

38. What is the term used to describe the natural increase of land?

    A. Expansion
    B. Avulsion
    C. Erosion
    D. Accretion

39. What is the length of time allowed for depreciation for a residential property?

    A. 5 years
    B. 27.5 years
    C. 39 years
    D. 70 years

40. What is the term used to describe personal property?

    A. Chattel
    B. Investment
    C. Possession
    D. Real property

41. Which act was enacted to ensure parties involved in a real estate transaction receive complete settlement cost disclosure?

    A. RESPA
    B. FHA
    C. Clean Water Act
    D. Civil Rights Act

42. What is the name given to the downward movement of water through soil?

    A. Absorption
    B. Filtration
    C. Percolation
    D. Proration

43. What type of income is generated by investing in a limited partnership?

    A. Active income
    B. Passive income
    C. Surplus income
    D. Savings

44. What mortgage type allows the mortgagor to make payments only on the interest accrued?

    A. Blanket mortgage
    B. Balloon mortgage
    C. Graduated mortgage
    D. Straight term mortgage

45. Mary's agent helped her purchase a property and negotiated a mortgage for her. This agent also represented the seller. What type of agent did Mary engage?

    A. Single agent
    B. Dual agent
    C. Double agent
    D. None of the above

46. What is the land survey process that involves the surveyor starting at an easily identifiable point and describing the property in terms of courses and distances and eventually returning to the starting point?

    A. ALTA
    B. Boundary construction
    C. Metes and bounds
    D. Topographic surveys

47. What arrangement allows the seller to absorb an existing loan in order to allow the buyer another mortgage?

    A. Simple mortgage
    B. Wraparound mortgage
    C. Mortgage by conditional sale
    D. Reverse mortgage

48. Which real estate participants are legally required to be licensed?

    A. Sellers
    B. Buyers
    C. Lenders
    D. Real estate agents and brokers

49. What is the term used to refer to the act of mixing money belonging to a client with one's own funds?

A. Commingling
B. Investing
C. Stealing
D. Saving

50. What is the effect of a larger money supply on the interest rates?

A. They decrease
B. They increase
C. Remains constant
D. They have no relationship

51. What is a homeowner's policy that covers two parts: property and liability?

A. HO1
B. HO2
C. HO3
D. HO4

52. What is the name given to tax calculated based on the value of an asset?

A. Ad valorem tax
B. Property tax
C. Capital gains tax
D. Transfer tax

53. What kind of lease agreement requires the landlord to pay for all expenses?

A. Gross lease
B. Ground lease
C. Net lease
D. Sublease

54. If a seller nets $442,000 from the sale of her home, and the commission is 5%, how much did the home sell for?

A. $464,100
B. $420,952
C. $459,680
D. None of the above

55. What is the short-term loan that covers the interval between selling one property and buying another?

A. Bridge Loan
B. Cash flow
C. Cash on cash return
D. Mortgage

56. What are the set rules established for condominium or co-op tenants?

A. House rules
B. Investment agreement
C. Regulations
D. Policy

57. Who is responsible for the rent in a sublease?

   A. New tenant
   B. Lessee
   C. Lessor
   D. Roommate

58. What income type does a salary fall under?

   A. Active income
   B. Passive income
   C. Savings
   D. Investment

59. What is the name given to an estate that gives the holder temporary possession rights?

   A. Concurrent estates
   B. Estate for years
   C. Freehold estates
   D. Leasehold estate

60. What is a permit issued to a builder stating the property is fit for occupancy?

   A. Certificate of occupancy
   B. Contract of sale
   C. Landmark designation
   D. Receipt of sales deposit

61. What kind of mortgage pays off the principal?

   A. Amortized loan
   B. Fixed- rate loan
   C. Floating rate loan
   D. Mortgage

62. What is the income that is left after all operating costs are paid in a real estate investment?

   A. Investment
   B. Net operating income
   C. Profit
   D. Revenue

63. Which lease allows for changes in rent within the lease term?

   A. Graduated lease
   B. Lease break
   C. Sublease
   D. Value point

64. What is the married couple's capital gains tax exclusion on the sale of their primary home?

   A. $50,000
   B. $75,000
   C. $250,000
   D. $500,000

65. What should a licensee do with their pocket card?

    A. Advertise it
    B. Carry a physical copy or have a digital image on a device
    C. File it
    D. Use it to get clients

66. You must have a real estate license for all of the following activities **EXCEPT**:

    A. Selling a mobile home not affixed to the land
    B. Selling a commercial property
    C. Selling a residential property
    D. Representing a client who wants to rent

67. What is a single person's capital gains tax exclusion?

    A. $25,000
    B. $100,000
    C. $250,000
    D. $500,000

68. What is the term given to violation of neighbor's property by trespassing?

    A. Easement
    B. Escheat
    C. Encroachment
    D. Encumbrance

69. What type of insurance is referred to as renter's insurance?

    A. HO1
    B. HO2
    C. HO3
    D. HO4

70. What is a form of co-ownership by which all parties have undivided interests in the property but no right of survivorship?

    A. Tenancy in common
    B. Tenancy in entirety
    C. Joint tenancy
    D. Ownership in severalty

71. What conveys a grantor's interest in real property?

    A. Deed
    B. Insurance
    C. Title
    D. Warrant

72. What is the chain of deeds and other documents used in transferring title of land from one owner to another consecutively?

    A. Abstract of title
    B. Deed chain
    C. History of deed
    D. Chain of title

73. If you paid a down payment of $200,000 for a property worth $1,000,000 dollars and you currently rent it out for $4,000 a month, what is the cash on cash return?

    A. 4%
    B. 4.8%
    C. 20%
    D. 24%

74. What is a Certificate of Eligibility?

    A. Certificate that shows one is to be exempt from property tax
    B. Certificate that is presented by veterans to show proof that they have met the minimum service requirements to be eligible for a VA loan
    C. Certificate that shows a construction is fit for occupancy
    D. Certificate that shows merit

75. What is the insurance policy that protects a lender from loss due to disputes over ownership of a property and defects in the title?

    A. Hazard insurance
    B. Home warranty
    C. Homeowner's insurance
    D. Title insurance

76. Property that has a divided form of ownership is called?

    A. Cooperative
    B. Planned unit development
    C. Time-share
    D. Joint tenants

77. What is the definition of a syndication?

    A. Income that is earned by a spouse prior to marriage
    B. Land that is divided into smaller pieces of land
    C. Mutual funds that invest in rental properties
    D. Real estate that is purchased by a group which includes at least one sponsor and several investors

78. Which of the following is **not** an essential element of a contract?

    A. Notarized signature
    B. Consideration
    C. Agreement by offer and acceptance
    D. Competent parties

79. Which listing agreement allows the owner of the listed property to sell the property on their own and not have to pay commission to the listing broker?

    A. Open listing
    B. Option listing
    C. Exclusive agency listing
    D. Both A and C

80. What is the listing agreement that gives the broker the payment of commission no matter who sells the property?

    A. Entirety
    B. Exclusive-right-to-sell listing
    C. Open listing
    D. Net Listing

81. Which is an example of functional obsolescence?

   A. Four bedrooms and one bathroom in a private residence
   B. All bedrooms located on the 2nd floor and only one bathroom located on the 1st floor
   C. Walking through one bedroom to get to another bedroom
   D. All of the above

82. Which act was passed to protect consumers from being scammed when purchasing raw land?

   A. Interstate Land Sales Full Disclosure Act
   B. Federal Fair Housing Act
   C. Equal Credit Opportunity Act
   D. Federal Real Estate Law

83. Which statement is a listing agent required to reveal to a prospective buyer?

   A. The physical health of the previous owner
   B. Renovations made within the last 5 years
   C. Re-zoning of a property
   D. The number of members living in a home

84. Real estate taxes are based on the value of a home. A property owner can be taxed additionally to help pay for projects that benefit the neighborhood. What is this type of tax called?

   A. Property tax
   B. Special assessment tax
   C. Progressive tax
   D. Capital gains tax

85. Which anti-trust violation applies to real estate?

    A. Monopolization
    B. Price-fixing
    C. Collusion
    D. None of the above

86. A _____ transfers a title of real property without the owner's consent.

    A. Involuntary alienation
    B. Redlining
    C. Lien
    D. Deed restriction

87. Which of the following is a common-law fiduciary duty?

    A. Care
    B. Accounting
    C. Confidentiality
    D. All of the above

88. Which type of lease increases at specific intervals?

    A. Lease option
    B. Graduated lease
    C. Month to month lease
    D. Triple net lease

89. A _____ can be granted by a zoning board if a property owner demonstrates a need to deviate from the current zoning requirements.

   A. Variance
   B. Moratorium
   C. Quitclaim
   D. Encumbrance

90. A defect that is not apparent after an ordinary inspection is called a(n) _____.

   A. Undisclosed defect
   B. Material defect
   C. Arbitration
   D. Latent defect

91. Which of the following statement(s) is(are) true about an option to purchase agreement?

   A. The seller is required to accept any offer that meets all of their needs
   B. The buyer is required to buy the property once the option agreement has been completed
   C. The seller can change their mind about the offer if a better offer has been received
   D. All of the above

92. Which type of loan requires the debt ratio to not exceed 41%?

   A. Federal Housing Administration loan
   B. VA loan
   C. Interest-only mortgage
   D. Adjustable rate mortgage

93. What is the difference between a lien theory and a title theory?

    A.   Lien theory is when the title is held by the lender until the final payment is made

    B.   Title theory is when the title is held by the borrower

    C.   Lien theory is when the title is held by the borrower with a lien to the property granted to the lender

    D.   In title theory the borrower never holds the title

94. This type of loan is banned in 25 states and increases the principal balance of a loan because of a failure to make payments to the loan that covers the interest due?

    A.   Conventional loan

    B.   Negative amortization

    C.   Unsecured loan

    D.   Open-ended loan

95. Which of the following will terminate an agency in a broker-seller relationship?

    A.   The owner declares bankruptcy

    B.   The broker gets assistance from another broker to help sell the property

    C.   The owner moves out of the property

    D.   All of the above

96. Which type of community groups housing, recreation and commercial units into one self-contained development?

    A.   Timeshare

    B.   Mixed-use development

    C.   Cooperative

    D.   Planned unit development

97. A(an)_____ allows crops produced annually to be harvested from the owner or tenant who planted the crops even if the property was sold or the lease expired.

    A. Lis pendens
    B. Suit to partition
    C. Emblement
    D. Index lease

98. Which law requires lenders to disclose all loan costs to the borrower?

    A. Borrower Transparency Act
    B. Regulation Z
    C. Fair Housing Act
    D. Federal Trade Commission

99. This is the largest real estate organization in the United States.

    A. National Association of Realtors
    B. The Realtors Association
    C. United States Realtors Association
    D. None of the above

100. Which of the following factors affects real estate supply?

    A. Labor force
    B. Government controls
    C. Construction costs
    D. All of the above

THIS IS THE END OF THE NATIONAL PORTION.

State Portion

1. Which of the following types of ownership is not recognized in the state of Georgia?

   A. Tenancy by entirety
   B. Joint tenancy
   C. Sole ownership
   D. All of the above are recognized

2. Person A enters into a contract to buy a timeshare in the state of Georgia. He then decides he does not want to buy the timeshare. Person A has how many days, after entering into the contract to rescind the contract?

   A. 5 days
   B. 7 days
   C. 1 day
   D. Once the contract has been signed, he cannot rescind the contract

3. If a seller does not have a copy of the warranty deed, it can be found at the _____.

   A. County courthouse
   B. Local housing development office
   C. GREC office
   D. The seller must keep the document at hand

4. Georgia states that a mobile home fixed to land is considered _____.

   A. Personal property
   B. Real estate
   C. Industrial real estate
   D. Commercial real estate

5. The first corner that is surveyed in the metes and bounds method of a legal description is called _____.

   A. The point of beginning
   B. The starting point
   C. The beginning of the survey
   D. There is no name for this

6. Which of the following statements is true regarding intangible taxes?

   A. It is negotiable between the buyer and seller
   B. The federal government imposes this tax
   C. The licensed realtor is required to pay this tax
   D. All of the above is true

7. Georgia's homestead protection laws do which of the following?

   A. Protect property from eminent domain
   B. Provide low interest mortgages from specified groups of people
   C. Protect a small parcel of property from creditors and adverse possession laws
   D. None of the above

8. Georgia requires _____ of occupation for a person to claim adverse possession of property.

   A. 20 years
   B. 10 years
   C. 5 years
   D. 30 years

9. Which of the following statements is true regarding discrimination against tenants, in the state of Georgia?

   A. Landlords can discriminate based on religion
   B. Discrimination within the scope of providing affordable and accessible housing for older people is legal
   C. There are no discrimination laws in the state of Georgia
   D. None of the above is true

11. What is the statute of limitation for written contracts in the state of Georgia?

   A. 1 year
   B. 2 years
   C. 4 years
   D. 6 years

10. Georgia requires rental deposits to be returned to the tenant within _____ of termination.

   A. 90 days
   B. 1 year
   C. 30 days
   D. 15 days

12. The _____ is not required in the state of Georgia, but the law requires a seller to inform the buyer about any known defects.

   A. Home defect form
   B. Buyer's information form
   C. Seller's disclosure
   D. All of these forms are required

13. A modification of a will is called a(n)
     _____.

     A. Arbitration
     B. Codicil
     C. Easement
     D. Appurtenance

14. The Georgia statute of frauds states that
     contracts must be _____ in order to be
     enforceable

     A. In writing
     B. Witnessed by a lawyer
     C. Verbally or in writing
     D. Signed by a state employee

15. The GREC has the right to _____ for not
     notifying the commission of an address
     change and opening or closing of trust
     accounts within 30 days.

     A. Permanently revoke a license
     B. Suspend a license
     C. Charge a penalty fee
     D. Enforce additional education

16. A _____ is a recorded legal document that
     gives constructive notice that action is
     being taken against a specified parcel of
     land.

     A. Dominant tenement
     B. Lis pendens
     C. Arbitration
     D. Servient tenement

17. Georgia is a _____, which means the borrower retains the title with the express agreement that the lender can take back the title if the borrower defaults on the loan.

    A.   Intermediary theory state
    B.   Deed of reconveyance
    C.   Lien theory state
    D.   Title theory state

18. What is a usury?

    A.   Charging additional penalties for paying more than the minimum on a loan
    B.   A licensee charging more commission than legally allowed
    C.   A client refusing to pay commission on a home sold or bought
    D.   Charging interest in excess of the maximum rate legally allowed

19. Georgia requires which of the following to claim adverse possession?

    A.   Be in actual possession of the property
    B.   Be non-permissive of the property
    C.   Use property in an "open and notorious" way
    D.   All of the above are requirements

20. The Georgia Timeshare Act requires developers to make disclosures to perspective buyers such as the number of days they have to rescind a contract. This information would be contained in the _____.

    A.   Promissory note
    B.   Purchase agreement
    C.   Public offering statement
    D.   Seller's disclosure statement

21. The _____ is when the title to the property is acquired after the owner attempts to sell or transfer to another before they actually get the title.

    A. After Acquired Sale
    B. Doctrine of After Acquired Title
    C. Delayed title
    D. None of the above

22. Which of the following is not true regarding the covenants of warranty?

    A. Applied for all of time
    B. There are 6 covenants of warranty
    C. Covenant of seisin means that the property is not subject to any outstanding rights or interests or other parties
    D. All of the above are true

23. This type of deed is a deed that conveys real property without covenants.

    A. Bargain and sale deeds
    B. Grant deed
    C. General warranty deed
    D. Quit claim deed

24. _____ is when actual knowledge of the matter has been conveyed to the recipient.

    A. Constructive notice
    B. Sufficient notice
    C. Legal notice
    D. Actual notice

25. A real property deed needs to recorded immediately with the _____.

    A. State department
    B. GREC
    C. County clerk in the county where the property is located
    D. Local commissioner's office

26. _____ is when a lender refuses to approve a loan only because of the particular neighborhood involved.

    A. Redlining
    B. Blacklisting
    C. Arbitration
    D. Reconveyance

27. Georgia requires the amount of commission to be paid to a broker to be _____.

    A. Stated in the contract
    B. A fixed percentage in the entirety of the state
    C. A fixed amount in the entirety of the state
    D. Dependent on experience of the broker

28. To enforce a commission, claim in Georgia, the first thing a broker is required to prove in court is _____.

    A. That they held a valid real estate licensee at the time they earned the commission
    B. That the principal did not pay a commission
    C. That they are a member of the GREC
    D. None of the above

29. In Georgia, the license activation fee for a firm is _____.

   A. $45
   B. $20
   C. 5% of total commission earned
   D. $75

30. The _____ is used to define property lines in Georgia.

   A. Property maps
   B. Georgia Militia Districts
   C. Mete and Bounds
   D. Plat maps

31. During its regularly scheduled first monthly meeting the GREC needs to select a _____.

   A. Chairperson
   B. Vice Chairperson
   C. Commissioner
   D. A&B only

32. Which of the following is a direct violation of the Georgia Real Estate License Law?

   A. A licensee refusing to accept a listing due to the owner's minority status
   B. A licensee refusing a listing because they are not taking more clients
   C. A licensee telling a principal of all offers no matter how low the offer is
   D. All of the above are violations of the Georgia Real Estate License Law

33. In an exclusive agency listing the seller must pay commission to the listing agent except when the property is sold by _____.

   A. A perspective buyer
   B. Another agent
   C. The owner's personal efforts
   D. The owner must always pay commission

34. Where can chain of title can be found in the state of Georgia?

   A. County commissioner's office
   B. GREC offices
   C. The current owner of the property must keep it
   D. County clerk's office

35. Which of the following is an example of constructive notice?

   A. Private letters mailed to homeowners in a specific development
   B. Legal notice posted on a public forum
   C. Notice given by an attorney
   D. All of the above are examples

36. This type of deed is used when an officer of the court needs to convey a title.

   A. Deed of trust
   B. Deed of reformation
   C. Court ordered deed
   D. Gift deed

37. A licensee who has been convicted of a felony must _____.

   A. Surrender their license within 30 days
   B. Quit the brokerage they are working at
   C. Notify the commission immediately
   D. None of the above is true

38. If a licensee is aggrieved by a final decision in a contested case, they are entitled to a judicial review in accordance with the _____.

   A. Georgia Administrative Procedures Act
   B. Federal Administrative Procedures Act
   C. Georgia Judicial Review Act
   D. Federal Judicial Review Act

39. The Real Estate Education, Research, and Recovery Fund must maintain a minimum balance, in order to maintain this the GREC has the authority assess each licensee an amount not to exceed _____.

   A. $100
   B. $30
   C. $75
   D. $25

40. In order for a claimant to collect damages from the Real Estate Education, Research, and Recovery Fund the claimant must have _____.

   A. Received a valid judgement from a court of competent jurisdiction
   B. Filed a claim against the licensee within 5 years
   C. Notified the licensee of the judgement
   D. All of the above must be done

41. A licensee is transferring to another brokerage. The application for transfer requires which of the following?

    A. The signature of the transferring licensee
    B. The approval of the previous brokerage
    C. A signed affidavit
    D. All of the above

42. An internet advertisement requires which of the following in the state of Georgia?

    A. Name of the licensee's firm
    B. Phone number of the licensee's firm
    C. Cost and square footage of properties being advertised
    D. A&B only

43. Georgia requires brokerages that use a trade name on sale signs or business cards to include _____.

    A. The name of the licensee
    B. The license number of the brokerage
    C. The firm's name that has been registered with the GREC
    D. All of the above

44. GREC revokes a broker's license. What happens to the sales associate's licenses?

    A. They are transferred to another broker or are placed on inactive status
    B. They can keep working under the broker completing transactions the broker worked on
    C. Their licenses are revoked
    D. Their licenses are suspended until an investigation can occur

45. A brokerage has a website to advertise their services. Any outdated information must be updated within _____ from the website.

    A. 90 days
    B. 30 days
    C. 15 days
    D. There are no rules regarding updated a brokerage's website

46. In Georgia, if a broker advertises a specific property for sale or rent, the advertisement must include _____.

    A. The name of the brokerage
    B. The address of the property
    C. The number of the brokerage
    D. A&C only

47. Georgia requires brokers to maintain a trust or escrow account. They must provide GREC with _____.

    A. The total amount in the account every month
    B. They do not have to provide GREC with anything
    C. The name of the bank and the number or name of the account
    D. A&C only

48. What is the total aggregate amount the Real Estate Education, Research and Recovery Fund will pay on behalf of a licensee?

    A. $100,000
    B. $75,000
    C. $50,000
    D. There is no total aggregate amount

49. A licensee is sued by a principal and has been required to pay the principal $15,000. The licensee owns a cabin in Georgia valued at $10,000, free, and clear. For the licensee to file a claim against the Real Estate Education, Research and Recovery Fund what must the licensee do first?

A. Attempt to give the home to the principal as payment
B. Have the property levied upon, sold, and file a claim against the Real Estate Education Research, and Recovery Fund for the remaining balance
C. The licensee does not have to do anything they can file a claim against the fund even if they have the capital
D. None of the above

50. Complaints against a licensee, received by GREC, must be within the last _____.

A. 90 days
B. 1 year
C. 5 years
D. 3 years

51. Which of the following is the process of a GREC investigation and hearing?

A. Investigation-complaint-hearing-final decision
B. Complaint-investigation-hearing-final decision
C. Complaint-lawsuit-investigation-hearing-final decision
D. Lawsuit-investigation-hearing-final decision

52. The commission has the right to _____ whose has been suspended or revoked.

A. Publish the name of the licensee on its' official website
B. Take away all commissions from that year
C. Allow the licensee to practice in in another county
D. All of the above

THIS IS THE END OF THE STATE PORTION.

Answer Key – National Portion

1.	A	21.	C	41.	A	61.	A	81.	D
2.	A	22.	A	42.	C	62.	B	82.	A
3.	D	23.	C	43.	B	63.	A	83.	C
4.	D	24.	A	44.	D	64.	D	84.	B
5.	D	25.	B	45.	B	65.	B	85.	B
6.	A	26.	A	46.	C	66.	A	86.	A
7.	B	27.	B	47.	B	67.	C	87.	D
8.	C	28.	C	48.	D	68.	C	88.	B
9.	C	29.	C	49.	A	69.	D	89.	A
10.	B	30.	A	50.	A	70.	A	90.	D
11.	A	31.	B	51.	C	71.	A	91.	B
12.	D	32.	D	52.	A	72.	D	92.	A
13.	D	33.	B	53.	A	73.	D	93.	C
14.	C	34.	A	54.	D	74.	B	94.	B
15.	D	35.	C	55.	A	75.	D	95.	A
16.	B	36.	B	56.	A	76.	C	96.	D
17.	C	37.	A	57.	B	77.	D	97.	C
18.	B	38.	D	58.	A	78.	A	98.	B
19.	D	39.	B	59.	D	79.	D	99.	A
20.	A	40.	A	60.	A	80.	B	100.	D

1.   **A) Pre-approval**

Prior to purchasing a property, the borrower can visit a lender and obtain a pre-approval letter stating the amount of credit the lender is willing to accord the buyer which will help determine what the buyer can afford.

2.   **A) Usable Square Footage**

Usable square footage is the amount of space you actually occupy in a leased space.

3.   **D) Principal**

The principal is the amount of money that a lender gives a borrower to facilitate property purchase. Payment of principal results in increase in borrower's equity.

4. **D) VA mortgage**

This is a mortgage plan that is tailored to assist service members and their surviving spouses to become homeowners. There are usually a lot of qualifying standards put in place to be eligible for this type of mortgage and it is usually offered by banks and other credit facilities. The Veteran administration usually acts as a guarantor for the loan. Qualified Veterans are usually eligible for 100% financing.

5. **D) Remaining term**

It is usually used to complete the period of time left on a loan and the amount of principal payment to be covered within that period.

6. **A) Leaseback**

This is an arrangement that allows a seller to lease a property from the purchaser on transfer of ownership. The details surrounding the lease arrangement are usually discussed immediately after the sale.

7. **B) Easement in gross**

Easement in gross is the agreement that attaches rights to the tenant over the property. Transfer of the land results in an immediate termination of the agreement. The agreement can be renegotiated with the new tenant over time.

8. **C) Prepayment penalty**

This is the penalty placed on the significant payment of a mortgage within the first five years of the loan. This penalty exists to protect lenders from loss of interest income.

9. **C) Private mortgage insurance**

These insurance payments are usually discontinued once a buyer builds up to 20% equity on the home.

10. **B) Third party originator**

This is any third party used to originate a loan. Lenders often employ the services of third-party moderators to underwrite and originate loans. They offer no ongoing and lasting responsibility for the mortgage.

11. **A) Capital Improvement**

This is the addition of a permanent change in a structure or restoration of damaged property. It is done to increase the longevity and market value of the property. For an item to be considered a capital investment, it has to be a permanent addition and capable of improving the value of the property.

12. **D) Transfer tax**

This is any tax that is levied on transfer of ownership or title of property from one individual to another. It is usually non-deductible. It is usually levied at the local or federal level depending on the type of property changing ownership.

13. **D) All of the above**

Sales Comparison Approach, Cost Approach, and Income Approach are all appraisal methods.

14. **C) One year**

An asset must be held for at least one year before selling in order for profits to be categorized as long-term capital gains.

15. **D) All of the above**

Operating expenses include any costs associated with the operation and maintenance of an income-producing property.

16. **B) Refusing to leave a property despite expiration or termination of lease**

Commonly compared to an eviction, which is the legal removal of an individual from a lease due to violation of the terms of the agreement.

17. **C) Rate lock**

This occurs when lenders lock in a rate because it is the lowest rate being offered at the time. It is not a legally binding agreement and borrowers are allowed to abandon the rates based on the rising and falling.

18. **B) Lease option**

A lease option is a lease agreement that gives the tenant a choice to purchase the property within or at the end of the lease. It gives the buyer flexibility to make a purchase on the property. Usually involves an upfront agreement between the tenant and the landlord.

19. **D) The cooling capacity of an air conditioner and is measured in tons**

It is determined by measuring the size of the space being serviced by the air conditioner. The size area of the room is measured and multiplied by 25 BTU to determine the cooling capacity required in an air conditioner.

20. **A) Mortgage broker**

This is an individual that serves as an intermediate between lenders and brokers. A mortgage broker facilitates negotiations of interest rates and takes circulation of paperwork between the lender and the borrowers.

21. **C) $350,000**

$105,000 / 0.3 = $350,000

22. **A) Notice to cure**

This is a notice given to a leaseholder by the landlord regarding participation in activities that are not allowed in the building. The tenant is given 10 days to correct the mistake. Refusal to make adjustment results in the tenant being served a notice of termination.

23. **C) Pitch**

Defines the steepness of a roof. It is used to determine the material used for roofing and the space in the attic. It is also used to determine stability so that corrective measures can be undertaken early.

24. **A) The client**

A broker is required to work in the best interests of the client to ensure the best possible deal for the client.

25. **B) Easement**

This is the right to use another person's land temporarily without actually possessing it.

26. **A) Disabled**

Disabled, veterans, elderly, farmers, Gold Star Parents, and Star Program Homeowners. The above classes of people can get partial tax exemption by having the values of their homes reduced translating in reduced property taxes.

27. **B) 18 years**

This is the minimum required age for a real estate agent that has taken the education course and passed the qualifying exam.

28. **C) Fuse**

A fuse is a small conductor that is designed to melt under high current to break the circuit. A fuse should always maintain a series connection to the component of the circuit.

29. **C) A contract that involves both a promisor and promisee**

This contract occurs when both parties exchange a promise for a promise. Both parties enter into an agreement to fulfill their side of the bargain. Each party is also an obligor and obligee in this type of contract.

30. **A) Assessed value**

Assessed value is the monetary value assigned to a property and is usually used to determine the value of a property for the purpose of taxation.

31. **B) Environmental Protection Agency**

The Environmental Protection Agency is tasked with protecting both human and environmental health. The agency creates standards and laws promoting health of individuals and the environment and participates in upholding them by administering correcting efforts like CERCLA.

32. **D) Pro Forma Statement**

This is an estimate summary of income production if the current trends are maintained. This is usually in multifamily properties in order to help the investor understand general financial operations of the property.

33. **B) Create record of refusal in writing**

In the case where a client refuses to sign a disclosure, the agent is required to clearly state the names of the client and the facts surrounding the refusal to sign the disclosure. An agent is also required to sign a declaration in the presence of a notary public and have it notarized.

34. **A) Mortgage**

A voluntary lien is a claim a debtor has over the property of another and is initiated by the debtor as in the case of a mortgage. The debtor cannot legally sell the property as it is considered collateral.

35.   **C) Broker**

An agent resorts to a broker for commission as the law does not allow salespersons to work independently and therefore cannot be paid directly. A broker on receiving commission from the sale of the property is required to split the commission amongst the agents that were involved in the transaction.

36.   **B) Ownership in severalty**

This is a situation where real estate is owned by a single person or entity providing the owner with the most control of the land. A sole owner is at will to take any action on the land such as selling or leasing.

37.   **A) People who pose as real estate clients to check if fair housing is being practiced**

Testing was initiated under the Fair Housing Act to ensure that housing providers act in accordance with the fair housing laws that protect against discrimination based on race, origin and gender.

38.   **D) Accretion**

This is the natural growth of a parcel of land due to mother nature. It occurs due to accumulation of soil on the shoreline of a water body. A decrease due to erosion is also possible.

39.   **B) 27.5 years**

Depreciation is the loss of value of a property due to age, wear and tear. A residential property can only declare depreciation after 27.5 years in order to reduce the value of the property and property tax on the property.

40.   **A) Chattel**

A chattel is a tangible property which is either mobile or immobile. However, this term cannot be used to describe real estate holdings.

41.   **A) RESPA**

The Real Estate Settling Procedures Act was developed in order to protect the parties involved in a real estate transaction from abuse during the settlement process. The act mandates lenders and brokers to disclose all matters crucial to the transaction service, settlement service and consumer protection laws

42.   **C) Percolation**

This is the process in which water reaches the subsoil and roots. The pore space present in soil acts as a medium for the water to percolate. The ability of water to move through soil is dependent on the soil texture and structure. Some soils allow water to move very deep into the ground which may result in mixing with underground water reservoirs.

43.   **B) Passive income**

This is income that is generated with minimal activity. It requires little to no effort to earn on a daily basis.

44.   **D) Straight term mortgage**

A straight term mortgage is a mortgage that allows the mortgagor to make monthly payments on the interest accrued throughout the mortgage's lifespan. The principal remains unpaid until a set date where it becomes due for payment in full.

45.   **B) Dual agent**

Mary's agent was able to perform the above transactions for her because he was working for both the Mary and the seller of the property.

46.   **C) Metes and bounds**

This is a legal principle of land description and uses natural and artificial landmarks as boundaries. It is often used to describe irregular tracts of land. Metes defines straight line distances while bounds defines a less regular but identifiable lines. Measurements from an original point that is a monument and metes and bounds are described taking into account the boundaries. The process is repeated until the surveyor returns to the original point.

47.   **B) Wraparound mortgage**

Wraparound mortgages are used to refinance property. They are mini loans that include the balance of the preexisting mortgage and an additional loan to cover the new property. The seller is granted a promissory note highlighting the amount due.

48.   **D) Real estate agents and brokers**

They need to be licensed as they legally represent clients, buyers and sellers, in transferring ownership of property.

49.   **A) Commingling**

This is a breach of trust that occurs when a representative of a client mixes individual funds with that of the client making it impossible to determine the amounts that belong to each individual.

50. **A) They decrease**

Money supply is influenced by supply and demand. An increase in the money supply will result in a decreased interest rate making it easier to borrow and vice versa. Therefore, money and interest rates have an inversely proportional relationship.

51. **C) HO3**

A home owner's policy is a property insurance that covers losses and damages done to the insured's house and assets within the home. It also provides liability coverage against accidents within the home.

52. **A) Ad valorem tax**

This is the tax levied by a municipality or local government entity based on assessed value. A public assessor is engaged to value the property in order to calculate the tax owed.

53. **A) Gross lease**

This is a flat rent fee that included all expenses associated with ownership. It is inclusive of incidental charges such as taxes, insurance and utilities. It is an uncommon lease as landlords are unaware of the utility charges that may be incurred by a tenant.

54. **D) None of the above**

$442,000 / (1 - 0.05) = $465,263

55. **A) Bridge Loan**

This is a short-term loan of up to one year that provides cash flow enabling an individual to meet current obligations while awaiting permanent financing. It is often used in real estate to purchase a new home while awaiting the sale of the old property.

56. **A) House rules**

These are set rules that have been put in place to ensure the comfort of the tenants living within the building. Violation of the house rules clause may result in eviction.

57. **B) Lessee**

The original tenant for rent as he/she is liable to the owner. In case of overdue rent by the new tenant, the original tenant is held accountable.

58. **A) Active income**

This is an income earned from performing services. Active participation is required to yield payment.

59. **D) Leasehold estate**

This is a lease that allows the tenant to have real property for an extended period of time. A time frame is agreed upon in the lease and the tenant is allowed to erect structures and profit from the business that has been established at the site.

60. **A) Certificate of occupancy**

This is a legal statement issued by the building department clearing a building for occupancy on meeting the building codes and other laws that surround the construction of a residential or commercial building. It can be obtained when a new building is constructed or an old building is repurposed.

61. **A) Amortized loan**

An amortized loan is a loan with a scheduled payment over a period of time that pays off the interest and principal. An amortized loan payment schedule focuses on paying off the interest and progresses into the principal.

62. **B) Net operating income**

This is a method used to value the income generating properties. To obtain the value, all expenses incurred during operations is subtracted to the total income produced by the property. To get the true value produced by the property, revenues earned must be included.

63. **A) Graduated lease**

A graduated lease is an agreement between the landlord and tenant that allows for periodic adjustment of monthly payments based on the market value of the property. It stands to benefit the landlord over a long period of time.

64. **D) $500,000**

In accordance with the Taxpayers Relief Act, a married couple is eligible for exclusion from capital gain tax for profits of up to $500,000. This is provided the property sold is a primary residence, they have been living in it for at least 2 years.

65. **B) Carry a physical copy or have a digital image on a device**

A pocket card is a pocket-sized license identifying the holder as a licensed agent. It contains a photo, name and business address of the holder.

66. **A) Selling a mobile home not affixed to the land**

If the mobile home is sitting on a leased lot, then it is considered as personal property and can therefore be sold like a car or other personal belongings.

67.   **C) $250,000**

According to the Taxpayers relief act, a single person is eligible for a capital gains tax exemption for profits of up to $250,000 on the sale of a primary home.

68.   **C) Encroachment**

Encroachment is a violation of property rights that occurs when an individual chooses to ignore set boundaries. This can be by extending structure into the neighbor's land or illegally entering the neighbor's property.

69.   **D) HO4**

This insurance is designed to protect the insured and belongings from the covered losses. It covers liability, personal property, additional living expenses and medical payments to others. The insurance covers against risks specified in the policy.

70.   **A) Tenancy in common**

A tenancy in common is a legal agreement where two or more people with undivided rights own a property. Members of a tenancy in common are not mandated to have equal rights and can enter the agreement at any time. Members of a tenancy in common are free to leave their shares to a beneficiary.

71.   **A) Deed**

This is a signed legal document that conveys interest of a property and is used in cases of transfer of property provided a set of conditions are met. For a deed to hold legal merit, it must be filed in a public record.

72.   **D) Chain of title**

This is an official ownership record of a property. It is usually maintained from a centralized registry. It is used widely to protect lenders and buyers from losses occurring due to errors in the title report.

73.   **D) 24%**

($4,000 * 12) / $200,000 = 0.24

74.   **B) Certificate that is presented by veterans to show proof that they have met the minimum service requirements to be eligible for a VA loan**

The Certificate of Eligibility serves as proof of a veteran's military service and must be provided to lenders during the VA loan process

158

75. **D) Title insurance**

A title insurance is based on the indemnity clause. It is taken by a buyer to protect the lender from loss caused by unidentified defects in the title. It acts against traditional insurance by protecting clients against claims on a past occurrence

76. **C) Time-share**

Also called vacation ownership, a time-share is shared ownership of a property. This type of property is typically a vacation property i.e. a condominium in a resort area. The buyer typically purchases a certain period of time for the unit, typically one- to two-week periods.

77. **D) Real estate that is purchased by a group which includes at least one sponsor and several investors**

Syndication is a method investors can use to invest in properties. Investors pool their financial and intellectual resources together to invest in properties that they would not be able to invest in individually.

78. **A) Notarized signature**

A notarized signature is not necessary in a contract. A legal purpose, competent parties, offer and acceptance, consideration and consent are the essential elements of a contract.

79. **D) Both A and C**

Exclusive agency listing is an agreement between a real estate firm and seller which grants the firm the exclusive rights to sell the property but also allows the seller to sell the home without paying a commission to the listing agent. An open listing is a property listing using multiple real estate agents. This type of listing also allows an owner to list and sell the property without paying a commission to an agent.

80. **B) Exclusive-right-to-sell listing**

A legal agreement under which the seller agrees to pay a commission to the listing broker. The listing broker acts as the agent and is provided commission whether the property is sold through the listing broker, seller or anyone else. An exception occurs when the seller names one or more individuals/entities as exemptions in the listing agreement.

81. **D) All of the above**

Functional obsolescence occurs when an objects usefulness or desirability has been reduced because of an outdated design feature. They are features that cannot be easily fixed.

82.   **A) Interstate Land Sales Full Disclosure Act**

Passed in 1968, this act protects against land scams by facilitating the regulation of interstate land sales. Developers need to register subdivisions that contain more than 100 or more nonexempt lots. They may also provide purchasers with a disclosure statement (property report) prior to a sale.

83.   **C) Re-zoning of a property**

A seller is required to disclose all known material facts regarding the property to a buyer. Personal information about the family is not required but a re-zoning of the property must be disclosed.

84.   **B) Special assessment tax**

Property owners are sometimes taxed for improvements that effect some of the property owners within a taxing district. Only the property owners who have been affected will be taxed. These taxes pay for local infrastructure projects such as sewer lines, or construction and maintenance of roads.

85.   **B) Price-fixing**

Price-fixing, boycotting and allocation of customer or markets are the most common anti-trust violations in real estate.

86.   **A) Involuntary alienation**

This type of alienation results from a levy and sale for taxes that are due from the owner. It can also result from bankruptcy or an insolvency.

87.   **D) All of the above**

A fiduciary duty is an obligation to act in the best interest of the principal. There are 6 common law duties care, obedience, loyalty, disclosure, accounting and confidentiality.

88.   **B) Graduated lease**

This type of lease allows the landlord to a periodic adjustment of monthly payments. An increase in monthly payments could be due to market conditions or because of increase in the value of leased property.

89.   **A) Variance**

A variance is a request to deviate from current zoning requirements. It allows the owner to use a piece of land in a way that it is not usually permitted by the zoning ordinance. It is a waiver and does not change the zoning law.

90. **D) Latent defect**

A latent defect is a fault in a property that cannot be found through a reasonable inspection prior to a sale. These hazards may jeopardize the structural integrity or the occupant's safety.

91. **B) The buyer is required to buy the property once the option agreement has been completed**

In an option to buy agreement the buyer needs to purchase the property if the optionee agrees to the contract. The optionee is not required accept the buyers offer.

92. **A) Federal Housing Administration loan**

The FHA loan is designed for low to moderate borrowers and require a lower minimum down payments and credit score than other conventional loans. This type of loan is issued by an approved lender and insured by the FHA.

93. **C) Lien theory is when the title is held by the borrower with a lien to the property granted to the lender**

The difference between lien theory and title theory is that in lien theory the buyer holds the deed while in title theory the lender holds the title until the final payment is made.

94. **B) Negative amortization**

Negative amortization is banned in 25 states and is considered predatory by the federal government. It refers to increasing the principal balance of a loan due to the failure to cover the interest that is due on that loan.

95. **A) The owner declares bankruptcy**

When a property owner declares bankruptcy the agency agreement is terminated. If the principal passes, then the agreement is also terminated. Getting help from other brokers and moving out of the property are not means for termination.

96. **D) Planned unit development**

The planned unit development is a type of development that has varied, and compatible land uses i.e. housing, recreations and commercial centers.

97. **C) Emblements**

Emblements are considered personal property. It allows whoever planted the crops the ability to harvest them no matter who owns the property.

98. **B) Regulation Z**

   This law gives the borrowers the right to cancel certain credit transactions. This law is also called the Truth-in-Lending Laws.

99. **A) National Association of Realtors**

   The NAR is an organization of real estate brokers that was created to promote the profession and foster professional behavior to its members. It has its own code of ethics that all members are required to adhere to.

100. **D) All of the above**

   All of the above factors affect the supply of real estate. The government financial policies will also affect the supply of real estate.

Answer Key – State Portion

1.	A	21.	B	41.	A
2.	B	22.	C	42.	D
3.	A	23.	A	43.	C
4.	B	24.	D	44.	A
5.	A	25.	C	45.	B
6.	A	26.	A	46.	D
7.	C	27.	A	47.	C
8.	A	28.	A	48.	B
9.	B	29.	D	49.	B
10.	C	30.	B	50.	D
11.	D	31.	D	51.	B
12.	C	32.	A	52.	A
13.	B	33.	C		
14.	A	34.	D		
15.	C	35.	B		
16.	B	36.	C		
17.	A	37.	C		
18.	D	38.	A		
19.	D	39.	B		
20.	C	40.	A		

1.	**A) Tenancy by entirety**

Sole ownership and tenancy in common are both recognized in the state of Georgia but tenancy by entirety is not recognized.

2.	**B) 7 days**

The Georgia Condominium Act allows a buyer of a condominium or a timeshare 7 days to rescind the contract.

3.	**A) County courthouse**

The record room in the courthouse, in the grantor grantee index, would be the first point of reference for this document. It is a good business practice from the licensed agent to take the legal description from the seller's warranty deed.

4.	**B) Real estate**

Property fixed within the boundaries of residential lots and vacant lands is considered real estate. Furniture, cars, and boats are considered personal property.

5.   **A) The point of beginning**

Metes and bounds is a method of land description that is used by surveyors. The point of beginning gives the direction and the distances of the boundaries.

6.   **A) It is negotiable between the buyer and seller**

The intangible tax in Georgia is $1.50 per five hundred based on the amount of the loan. It must be paid within 90 days and if it is not then a penalty can be imposed.

7.   **C) Protect a small parcel of property from creditors and adverse possession laws**

Homestead laws protect portions of property from creditors and adverse possession. Adverse possession laws allow continuous trespassers to gain title to an abandoned piece of land or real estate.

8.   **A) 20 years**

20 years of occupation is required in order for someone to claim adverse possession of property. They must also do it publicly and pay property taxes or act as if they have the right to possess the property.

9.   **B) Discrimination within the scope of providing affordable and accessible housing for older people is legal**

The state prohibits discrimination against tenants on the basis of race, color, religion, gender, disability, familial status, or national origin.

10.   **C) 30 days**

Deposits must be deposited in an escrow account and returned to the tenant within 30 days of termination. Damages may be subtracted and itemized.

11.   **D) 6 years**

The statute of limitations for written contracts is 6 years. It is 4 years for oral contracts.

12.   **C) Seller's disclosure**

Georgia does not require a seller's disclosure, but they do require the seller to follow out a specific disclosure form. The state also requires a seller to inform a buyer about any known material defects.

13. **B) Codicil**

A codicil is a legal addition or supplement that explains, modifies, or revokes a will or part of a will.

14. **A) In writing**

Georgia requires contracts to be in writing in order for them to be enforceable. It is known as the statute of frauds. This includes contracts for the sale of land.

15. **C) Charge a penalty fee**

The fee would be 25 dollars. A fee for a returned check is much higher at 100 dollars.

16. **B) Lis pendens**

It is Latin for litigation pending and once it is recorded, notice is given to the public that there is a litigation pending over a parcel of real property. The sale would be held subject to the outcome of the litigation.

17. **A) Intermediary theory state**

In this type of jurisdiction, the borrower keeps the title with the agreement that the lender has the power to take back the title when the borrower defaults on the loan.

18. **D) Charging interest in excess of the maximum rate legally allowed**

The practice of usury is illegal. It is when a lender lends money at an interest rate that is considered unreasonably high.

19. **D) All of the above are requirements**

All of the above are necessary to claim adverse possession in the state of Georgia. The person must also continuously use the property and exclusively use the property.

20. **C) Public offering statement**

This document is provided to buyers of a new condominium or timeshare. It contains the details of how the building is structured and managed including the CC&Rs.

21. **B) Doctrine of After Acquired Title**

This protects the grantee will have title to the property even if they get the title at a later time.

22. **C) Covenant of seisin means that the property is not subject to any outstanding rights or interests or other parties**

    The covenant against encumbrances is a promise to the grantee that the property being conveyed is not subject to outstanding rights or interests such as mortgages, liens, and easements. The covenant for seisin is the same as the right to convey.

23. **A) Bargain and sale deed**

    This deed is used when property is transferred pursuant to a foreclosure, tax sale or settlement of the estate of a deceased person.

24. **D) Actual notice**

    This type of notice is delivered in a way that legally gives sufficient assurance actual knowledge of the matter has been conveyed to this recipient.

25. **C) County clerk in the county where the property is located**

    The recording of deed gives notice to all future buyers of who owned the property. The deed provides a formal title in exchange for money.

26. **A) Redlining**

    Redlining is an illegal practice of a beneficiary refusing a loan solely on the basis of the particular neighborhood involved. This is prohibited by the Federal Fair Housing Law.

27. **A) Stated in the contract**

    Commission is not a fix amount or percentage and can vary from licensee to licensee. It also must be listed in the contract with a principal.

28. **A) That they held a valid real estate licensee at the time they earned the commission**

    The broker and any salesperson involved in the transaction must prove that they had a valid real estate license at the time they earned the commission.

29. **D) $75**

    It is 75 dollars for a firm and 45 dollars for an individual person. 20 dollars of that activation fee goes to the real estate education, research, and recovery fund.

30. **B) Georgia Militia District**

    These military districts were formed many years ago to raise manpower and now those lines are used to define property.

31. **D) A&B only**

    The commission needs to select a chairperson and vice chairperson by secret ballot on the first meeting of the month.

32. **A) A licensee refusing to accept a listing due to the owner's minority status**

    This is considered as a direct violation of the Georgia Real Estate License Law.

33. **C) The owner's personal efforts**

    This type of listing is an agreement is exclusive to a specific firm or agent, but the seller still retains the right to market and sell the home to a buyer without being obligated to pay a commission to the listing agent.

34. **D) County clerk's office**

    The county clerk's office, where the property is located, is where the chain of title would be located. The chain of title is a recording of all the buyers and sellers of the specified piece of property.

35. **B) Legal notice posted in a public forum**

    This type of notice is an idea that a person can be notified by a public posting of pending legal action.

36. **C) Court ordered deed**

    These deeds are often issued as a result of legal proceedings and is used when an officer needs to convey a title.

37. **C) Notify the commission immediately**

    The commission must be notified immediately, by the licensee, of a felony offense conviction.

38. **A) Georgia Administrative Procedures Act**

    This law governs procedures for state administrative agencies to propose and issue regulations as well as provide for judicial review of agency adjudications and other final decisions in Georgia.

39. **B) $30**

    The GREC can require licensees to pay up to $30 additional dollars in fees to maintain the minimum required in the recovery fund. This additional fee must be paid upon renewal of license.

40.   **A) Received a valid judgement from a court of competent jurisdiction**

The claimant must have received a valid judgement from court stating that the licensee must pay damages in a specified amount. This is required to collect damages from the recovery fund.

41.   **A) The signature of the transferring licensee**

The application requires the signature of the transferring licensee in order to transfer the license to another company.

42.   **D) A&B only**

The name and phone number of the licensee's firm is required on every page of the website or advertisement.

43.   **C) The firm's name that has been registered with the GREC**

The firms registered trade name is required on any sale signs, business cards, contracts or other document that are related to a real estate transaction.

44.   **A) They are transferred to another broker or are placed on inactive status**

The licensees working under the broker needs to either transfer to another broker or they need to apply to place the license on inactive status, within one month of the broker's license being revoked.

45.   **B) 30 days**

Outdate information on a website of a brokerage or licensee needs to be updated or removed from the website within 30 days.

46.   **D) A&C only**

Georgia requires all advertisements specific to a property to also state the name of the brokerage or firm and the number of the firm or brokerage that has been registered with the commission.

47.   **C) The name of the bank and the number or name of the account**

This information must be provided by the broker to GREC within one month of opening the account.

48.   **B) $75,000**

The maximum the recovery fund will pay on behalf of a licensee is $75,000. After that has been exhausted the fund is not liable for future acts of that licensee.

49. **B) Have the property levied upon, sold, and file a claim against the Real Estate Education Research, and Recovery Fund for the remaining balance**

If a salesperson owes money through a lawsuit, they can only file a claim against the recovery fund if they do not have the funds to pay the lawsuit. In this example the property is fully owned by the licensee and there is no loan on it, so the licensee must sell it and pay the lawsuit first.

50. **D) 3 years**

When the GREC receives a sworn written request for investigation of a licensee they must investigate the actions. But the actions must have occurred within 3 years.

51. **B) Complaint-investigation-hearing-final decision**

The process of an investigation and hearing is a complaint needs to be filed, then an investigation must occur, then a hearing occurs and finally a decision is made regarding the complaint against a licensee.

52. **A) Publish the name of the licensee on its' official website**

The commission has the authority to publish the name of licensees whose license has been suspended or revoked on their website.

Practice Test 4

Directions:

1. You have a 4-hour time limit to complete the whole exam.

2. To pass, aim to answer at least 75 out of 100 questions correctly on the national portion **AND** at least 39 out of 52 questions on the state portion.

3. Some questions will require mathematics. You may use a calculator.

4. **Phones and pagers are not allowed. Having either will result in automatic dismissal from the exam and nullification of exam scores.**

Tips:

*   Answer all questions even if you are unsure.
*   Mark any questions you are stuck on and revisit them after you are done. The exam is timed so make sure you finish as many questions as you can.
*   After reading the question, try answering it in your head first to avoid getting confused by the choices.
*   Read the entire question before looking at the answers.
*   Use the process of elimination to filter out choices that don't seem correct to increase your chances of selecting the correct answer.
*   Be aware of important keywords like **not, sometimes, always,** and **never**. These words completely alter the ask of the question so it's important to keep track of them.

PLEASE READ THESE INSTRUCTIONS CAREFULLY.

Name: Belinda

Practice Test 4

NATIONAL PORTION

70/100

Date: _____

1. ✓ Ⓐ Ⓑ Ⓒ ●
2. ✓ Ⓐ Ⓑ Ⓒ ●
3. ✓ Ⓐ ● Ⓒ Ⓓ
4. ✓ ● Ⓑ Ⓒ Ⓓ
5. ✓ Ⓐ Ⓑ Ⓒ ●
6. ✓ ● Ⓑ ● Ⓓ
7. ✓ Ⓐ Ⓑ ● Ⓓ
(8.) D Ⓐ ● Ⓒ Ⓓ
9. B Ⓐ Ⓑ Ⓒ ●
10. ✓ Ⓐ ● Ⓒ Ⓓ
11. A Ⓐ Ⓑ Ⓒ ●
12. D Ⓐ Ⓑ ● Ⓓ
13. B ● Ⓑ Ⓒ Ⓓ
14. ✓ ● Ⓑ Ⓒ Ⓓ
15. ✓ Ⓐ ● Ⓒ Ⓓ
16. ✓ Ⓐ ● Ⓒ Ⓓ
(17) C ● Ⓑ Ⓒ Ⓓ
18. C Ⓐ Ⓑ Ⓒ ●
19. ✓ Ⓐ Ⓑ Ⓒ ●
20. Ⓐ Ⓑ Ⓒ ●
21. ✓ Ⓐ ● Ⓒ Ⓓ
22. ✓ ● Ⓑ Ⓒ Ⓓ
23. B Ⓐ Ⓑ Ⓒ ●
24. ✓ ● Ⓑ Ⓒ Ⓓ
25. B Ⓐ Ⓑ ● Ⓓ
26. ✓ Ⓐ Ⓑ Ⓒ ●
27. ✓ ● Ⓑ Ⓒ Ⓓ
28. A Ⓐ ● Ⓒ Ⓓ
29. C Ⓐ Ⓑ Ⓒ ●
30. ✓ Ⓐ Ⓑ ● Ⓓ

31. C Ⓐ Ⓑ Ⓒ Ⓓ
32. ✓ Ⓐ Ⓑ Ⓒ ●
33. B Ⓐ Ⓑ ● Ⓓ
34. ✓ Ⓐ ● Ⓒ Ⓓ
35. ✓ Ⓐ Ⓑ Ⓒ ●
36. B Ⓐ Ⓑ Ⓒ Ⓓ
37. ✓ Ⓐ Ⓑ ● Ⓓ
38. ✓ Ⓐ Ⓑ ● Ⓓ
39. ✓ ● Ⓑ Ⓒ Ⓓ
40. ✓ Ⓐ Ⓑ Ⓒ ●
41. ✓ Ⓐ Ⓑ Ⓒ ●
42. ✓ Ⓐ Ⓑ ● Ⓓ
43. B Ⓐ ● Ⓒ Ⓓ
44. ✓ Ⓐ ● Ⓒ Ⓓ
45. ✓ Ⓐ ● Ⓒ Ⓓ
46. ✓ ● Ⓑ Ⓒ Ⓓ
47. ✓ Ⓐ ● Ⓒ Ⓓ
48. ✓ ● Ⓑ Ⓒ Ⓓ
49. ✓ ● Ⓑ Ⓒ Ⓓ
50. ✓ Ⓐ Ⓑ ● Ⓓ
51. ✓ Ⓐ Ⓑ ● Ⓓ
52. D Ⓐ Ⓑ Ⓒ Ⓓ
53. D ● Ⓑ Ⓒ Ⓓ
54. B Ⓐ Ⓑ Ⓒ ●
55. ✓ Ⓐ ● Ⓒ Ⓓ
56. ✓ ● Ⓑ Ⓒ Ⓓ
57. ✓ Ⓐ Ⓑ Ⓒ Ⓓ
58. ✓ Ⓐ ● Ⓒ Ⓓ
59. ✓ Ⓐ Ⓑ ● Ⓓ
60. ✓ Ⓐ ● Ⓒ Ⓓ

61. B Ⓐ Ⓑ ● Ⓓ
62. D Ⓐ Ⓑ Ⓒ Ⓓ
63. ✓ ● Ⓑ Ⓒ Ⓓ
64. ✓ Ⓐ ● Ⓒ Ⓓ
65. ✓ Ⓐ Ⓑ Ⓒ Ⓓ
66. ✓ Ⓐ ● Ⓒ Ⓓ
67. ✓ Ⓐ ● Ⓒ Ⓓ
68. ✓ ● Ⓑ Ⓒ Ⓓ
69. ✓ Ⓐ ● Ⓒ Ⓓ
70. ✓ Ⓐ Ⓑ ● Ⓓ
71. ✓ ● Ⓑ Ⓒ Ⓓ
72. ✓ Ⓐ Ⓑ ● Ⓓ
73. D ● Ⓑ Ⓒ Ⓓ
74. ✓ Ⓐ Ⓑ Ⓒ ●
75. ✓ ● Ⓑ Ⓒ Ⓓ
76. ✓ Ⓐ Ⓑ ● Ⓓ
77. A Ⓐ Ⓑ ● Ⓓ
78. C ● Ⓑ Ⓒ Ⓓ
79. ✓ ● Ⓑ Ⓒ Ⓓ
80. D Ⓐ Ⓑ ● Ⓓ
81. A Ⓐ Ⓑ ● Ⓓ
82. ✓ Ⓐ ● Ⓒ Ⓓ
83. ✓ Ⓐ Ⓑ ● Ⓓ
84. ✓ Ⓐ Ⓑ Ⓒ ●
85. ✓ ● Ⓑ Ⓒ Ⓓ
86. ✓ ● Ⓑ Ⓒ Ⓓ
87. ✓ Ⓐ ● Ⓒ Ⓓ
88. ✓ Ⓐ ● Ⓒ Ⓓ
89. d ● Ⓑ Ⓒ Ⓓ
90. C Ⓐ ● Ⓒ Ⓓ

91. B ● Ⓑ Ⓒ Ⓓ
92. ✓ Ⓐ Ⓑ ● Ⓓ
93. B Ⓐ Ⓑ ● Ⓓ
94. A Ⓐ Ⓑ ● Ⓓ
95. ✓ Ⓐ Ⓑ Ⓒ ●
96.   ● Ⓑ Ⓒ Ⓓ
97. ✓ Ⓐ ● Ⓒ Ⓓ
98. ✓ Ⓐ Ⓑ ● Ⓓ
99. ✓ Ⓐ Ⓑ Ⓒ ●
100. A Ⓐ Ⓑ Ⓒ ●

Practice Test 4

Practice Test 4

Name: Belinda

STATE PORTION

Date: _____

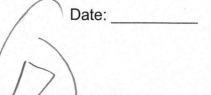

17

1. D ● Ⓐ Ⓑ Ⓒ Ⓓ
2. B Ⓐ Ⓑ Ⓒ Ⓓ
3.   Ⓐ Ⓑ Ⓒ ●
4. B Ⓐ Ⓑ Ⓒ Ⓓ
5. B ● Ⓑ Ⓒ Ⓓ
6. A Ⓐ Ⓑ Ⓒ ●
7.   Ⓐ Ⓑ Ⓒ ●
8.   Ⓐ ● Ⓒ Ⓓ
9. C Ⓐ ● Ⓒ Ⓓ
10.   Ⓐ Ⓑ Ⓒ ●
11.   Ⓐ ● Ⓒ Ⓓ
12. A Ⓐ Ⓑ ● Ⓓ
13. D ● Ⓑ Ⓒ Ⓓ
14.   Ⓐ Ⓑ ● Ⓓ
15.   ● Ⓑ Ⓒ Ⓓ
16.   Ⓐ Ⓑ Ⓒ ●
17.   Ⓐ Ⓑ ● Ⓓ
18.   Ⓐ Ⓑ Ⓒ ●
19. B Ⓐ Ⓑ ● Ⓓ
20.   Ⓐ ● Ⓒ Ⓓ
21. A Ⓐ ● Ⓒ Ⓓ
22.   Ⓐ Ⓑ ● Ⓓ
23.   Ⓐ Ⓑ Ⓒ ●
24. C Ⓐ Ⓑ Ⓒ ●
25. B ● Ⓑ Ⓒ Ⓓ
26.   Ⓐ Ⓑ Ⓒ ●
27. A ● Ⓑ Ⓒ Ⓓ
28.   Ⓐ ● Ⓒ Ⓓ
29.   ● Ⓑ Ⓒ Ⓓ
30. B Ⓐ Ⓑ Ⓒ ●

31. B Ⓐ ✗ Ⓒ ●
32.   Ⓐ Ⓑ ● Ⓓ
33. B Ⓐ Ⓑ ● Ⓓ
34. A Ⓐ Ⓑ Ⓒ ●
35.   Ⓐ Ⓑ ● Ⓓ
36.   ● Ⓑ Ⓒ Ⓓ
37. D Ⓐ Ⓑ Ⓒ ✗
38.   Ⓐ Ⓑ Ⓒ ●
39.   Ⓐ ● Ⓒ Ⓓ
40.   Ⓐ Ⓑ Ⓒ ●
41. A Ⓐ Ⓑ Ⓒ ●
42.   ● Ⓑ Ⓒ Ⓓ
43. B ● Ⓑ Ⓒ Ⓓ
44.   Ⓐ ● Ⓒ Ⓓ
45.   Ⓐ Ⓑ Ⓒ ●
46.   Ⓐ ● Ⓒ Ⓓ
47.   Ⓐ Ⓑ Ⓒ ●
48.   ● Ⓑ Ⓒ Ⓓ
49.   ● Ⓑ Ⓒ Ⓓ
50.   Ⓐ Ⓑ Ⓒ ●
51.   Ⓐ Ⓑ ● Ⓓ
52.   ● Ⓑ Ⓒ Ⓓ

Practice Test 4

National Portion

1. Which of the following is considered commercial real estate?

   A. Office building
   B. Warehouse
   C. Multifamily house
   D. All of the above

2. Jack is trying to convince Mary to move to a particular neighborhood because the residents there are of her ethnic background and religion. What is guilty of?

   A. Blockbusting
   B. Discriminating
   C. Convincing
   D. Steering

3. What type of lease would a tenant take when using a warehouse for the purpose of manufacturing and distribution?

   A. Gross lease
   B. Net lease
   C. Percentage lease
   D. Proprietary lease

4. What is a notice given on a pending lawsuit?

   A. Lis Pendens
   B. Statute of limitations
   C. Notice of intent
   D. Notice of default

5. Who issues variances?

   A. Architectural Review Board
   B. EPA
   C. Municipal Engineers
   D. Zoning Board of Appeals

6. What is the name given to an individual who originates, sells and services mortgage loans?

   A. Mortgage Banker
   B. Mortgage Broker
   C. Lender
   D. Borrower

7. What is the exterior layer of a house?

   A. Eaves
   B. Flashing
   C. Pitch
   D. Sheathing

8. Who holds on to the security deposit?

   A. Agent
   B. Broker
   C. Buyer
   D. Landlord

9. What is the term used to define the estimated age of a property based on its utilities and physical wear and tear?

   A. Economic life
   B. Effective age
   C. Use discount
   D. Depreciation

10. How long are brokers required to hold on to property files?

    A. One year
    B. Three years
    C. Five years
    D. Never

11. What is the unit used to measure furnace or air conditioner capacity?

    A. British Thermal Unit
    B. Bytes
    C. Joules
    D. Watts

12. What describes the type of estate granted within a lease?

    A. Acceleration clause
    B. Annuity law
    C. Cancellation clause
    D. Habendum clause

13. What type of income is income generated from a rental property?

    A. Active
    B. Passive
    C. Portfolio
    D. All the above

14. What is another name used to refer to land lease?

    A. Ground lease
    B. Home lease
    C. Percentage lease
    D. Estate lease

15. Which regulations govern the construction details of buildings with the sole interest of safeguarding the occupants and general public?

    A. APR
    B. Building codes
    C. Leasing laws
    D. Zoning codes

16. If a seller nets $325,000 from the sale of her home, and the commission is 3%, how much did the home sell for?

    A. $334,750
    B. $335,051
    C. $315,250
    D. $334,027

17. Personal property that is attached to real property, such as a chandelier, is regarded as

    A. An emblement
    B. An appliance
    C. A fixture
    D. A liability

18. What are outside amenities that maximize use of property called?

    A. Cosmetic improvements
    B. Essential improvements
    C. Offsite improvements
    D. Supplemental improvements

19. Which form of ownership passes the shares of ownership upon death?

    A. Life estate
    B. Severalty
    C. Tenancy in common
    D. Joint tenancy

20. If a property manager is fixing a leaky pipe, what type of maintenance is he doing?

    A. Aesthetic maintenance
    B. Appreciation
    C. Breakdown prevention
    D. Preventive maintenance

21. Which act was enacted in order to identify hazardous sites?

    A. Americans with disabilities Act
    B. CERCLA
    C. Fair Housing Act
    D. Civil Rights Act

22. What is tenancy in common?

    A. A shared tenancy in which each holder has a distinct, separately transferable interest
    B. A tenancy in which each holder has equal interest, where interest is automatically passed in case of death
    C. A tenancy in which interest is returned to the public upon death
    D. A tenancy in which a single owner owns full ownership of a property

23. What is the money available after deducting all expenses?

    A. Cash out returns
    B. Cash flow
    C. Cash on cash return
    D. Revenue

24. What is an involuntary lien?

    A. A lien that arises without the property owner's consent
    B. A lien that is initiated with owner's consent
    C. A lien that cannot be cashed on
    D. None of the above

25. What is the name given to property that legally qualifies as owner's principal property?

   A. Commercial property
   B. Homestead property
   C. Real property
   D. Personal property

26. A person authorized to handle a principal's affairs in one specific area is referred to as?

   A. General agent
   B. Dual agent
   C. Multi agent
   D. Special agent

27. What are real property rights conferred with ownership?

   A. Bundle of rights
   B. Right of first refusal
   C. Riparian rights
   D. Doctrine of equitable conversion

28. What is the fine placed for a violation of license law?

   A. $1,000
   B. $5,000
   C. $6,000
   D. $10,000

29. What is the term for commercial property depreciation?

   A. 5 years
   B. 29 years
   C. 39 years
   D. 40 years

30. The division of expenses at the time of closing between the buyer and seller in proportion to the actual use of a property is called?

   A. Bill of sale
   B. Loan to value ratio
   C. Proration
   D. Tax abatement

31. What is the equivalent of 1 cubic foot?

   A. 5.25 gallons
   B. 7.26 gallons
   C. 7.48 gallons
   D. 10 gallons

32. What is a statement that shows total revenues generated based on rent rolls and management styles?

   A. Invoice statement
   B. Income statement
   C. Pro forma statement
   D. Operating statement

33. What type of building is divided into two condominiums where the first is the co-op residential units (80%) and the second is for professional/commercial units (20%)?

    A. Condo
    B. Condop
    C. Co-op
    D. Multi family home

34. A person authorized to handle a principal's affairs in more than one specific area is referred to as?

    A. Special agent
    B. General Agent
    C. Dual agent
    D. Broker

35. What are the laws that limit the maximum interest rate that can be charged?

    A. APR
    B. Annuity laws
    C. FHA
    D. Usury

36. What is the nature of the title in co-op ownership?

    A. Freehold
    B. Leasehold
    C. Regular hold
    D. Lease assignment

37. What is a non-possessory interest in property giving a lienholder the right to foreclose?

    A. Mortgage
    B. Duties
    C. Taxes
    D. Revenue

38. What is the agreement that allows the tenant to continue living on a property once the lease has expired?

    A. Tenancy in common
    B. Tenancy in entirety
    C. Tenancy in sufferance
    D. Ownership in severalty

39. Can a salesperson hold other jobs?

    A. Yes
    B. No
    C. Only if it is in real estate
    D. Maybe

40. What does the Secondary Mortgage Market refer to in the loan process?

    A. Buyers that buy houses on mortgage
    B. Sellers that offer buy down arrangement
    C. Lending market
    D. Private investors and government agencies that buy and sell real estate mortgages

41. What are air rights?

    A. Right to breath
    B. Right to own an airspace
    C. Right to package air
    D. Rights granted to a property owner on the vertical space above the property

42. What is the relationship where agents work together in the best interest of their respective clients?

    A. Dual agency
    B. Single agency
    C. Co-broking
    D. Co-borrowing

43. What is the legal term for passing responsibility of your apartment onto another tenant?

    A. Sub lease
    B. Lease assignment
    C. Leasehold
    D. Lease break

44. If you have a loan of $200,000 with a 12% interest, how much do you pay in interest every month?

    A. $1,200
    B. $2,000
    C. $2,400
    D. $24,000

45. What are the extra charges above the selling costs that are incurred by the buyer on the purchase of a home?

    A. Common costs
    B. Closing costs
    C. Down payment
    D. Short fall

46. What are the monthly charges imposed on condo tenants?

    A. Common charges
    B. Common costs
    C. Service fees
    D. Short fall

47. What is the name given to the ratio defined by dividing monthly debt payments to gross monthly income?

    A. Loan to value ratio
    B. Debt to income ratio
    C. Earnest money deposit
    D. Foreclosure

48. What is the percentage amount of the selling price that is deposited by the buyer when closing a real estate transaction?

    A. Down payment
    B. Escrow
    C. Earnest money deposit
    D. Tax abatement

49. What is earnest money deposit?

   A. Money deposited by the buyer to the seller to show interest in the purchase of a home
   B. Purchase money
   C. Down payment
   D. Security deposit

50. What is the financial agreement that allows a third party to regulate payment where two parties are involved?

   A. Security deposit
   B. Sales deposit
   C. Escrow
   D. Earnest money deposit

51. What is the notice given when a tenant is in violation of the lease agreement and is up for eviction?

   A. Notice to cure
   B. Notice of intention
   C. Notice of termination
   D. Notice to quit

52. What is the notice given when a squatter is accommodated without the landlord's consent?

   A. Notice of default
   B. Notice of intention
   C. Notice to cure
   D. Notice to quit

53. What is the notice given to state that no work has been performed?

   A. Notice of cessation
   B. Notice given to evict an unruly tenant
   C. Notice filed in court by a lender on defaulting of payment
   D. Notice to discontinue the breach of lease within 10 days

54. What is the name given to a visit made to a potential property to identify the condition of the house?

   A. Final walk through
   B. Home inspection
   C. Appraisal
   D. Assessment

55. What mortgage plan allows a borrower to switch to a fixed-rate mortgage?

   A. Adjustable Rate Mortgage
   B. Convertible ARM
   C. Fixed rate mortgage
   D. Floating rate mortgage

56. What is the situation that arises when an individual that is legally required to make payments does not fulfill this obligation?

   A. Delinquency
   B. Defaulting
   C. Escalation clause
   D. Foreclosure

57. Which agency insures FHA-approved lenders?

   A. CERCLA
   B. Consumer Financial Protection Bureau
   C. Federal Emergency Management Agency
   D. Federal Housing Administration

58. Which agency is commissioned with overseeing products and services offered to consumers in the finance industry?

   A. Consumer Financial Protection Bureau
   B. Federal Housing Administration
   C. Environmental Protection Agency
   D. Federal Emergency Management Agency

59. What service allows brokers to share their listings?

   A. Broker Listing Service
   B. Single Agency Listing
   C. Multiple Listing Service
   D. Shared Listing Service

60. What is the contract covering household maintenance systems?

   A. Deed
   B. Home warranty
   C. Hazard insurance
   D. HO4

61. What is the name given to a real estate transaction where buyers outbid each other for the property?

   A. Acceleration clause
   B. Escalation clause
   C. Public auction
   D. Tender

62. What is the name given to a notice given showing interest in a property?

   A. Notice of cessation
   B. Notice to cure
   C. Notice of default
   D. Notice of intent

63. What is the increase in the value of a property?

   A. Appreciation
   B. Depreciation
   C. Obsolescence
   D. All of the above

64. What is the mortgage payment plan that involves making payments every fortnight?

   A. Balloon mortgage
   B. Biweekly mortgage
   C. Blanket mortgage
   D. Graduated mortgage

65. What term is used to describe the document attached to an original contract?

   A. Addendum
   B. Signed agreement
   C. Requirements clause
   D. Terms and conditions

66. What refinancing method allows a borrower to acquire cash from the transaction?

   A. Cash flow
   B. Cash out refinance
   C. Cash on cash return
   D. Refinancing

67. Who oversees that code restrictions are followed and construction / renovation are done by licensed professionals?

   A. Contractor
   B. Department of Buildings
   C. Zoning board
   D. Architectural Review Board

68. What is the final stage of a real estate transaction?

   A. Closing
   B. Sale
   C. Final walk through
   D. Handing of the title

69. What is the percentage of the selling price that is usually earned by a real estate agent for facilitating the transaction?

   A. Bonus
   B. Commission
   C. Salary
   D. Rent

70. What is the name of fees paid to the lender at closing in exchange for a reduced interest rate?

   A. Mortgage
   B. Service fee
   C. Discount points
   D. Principal fee

71. Which Act was passed to protect against discrimination in borrowing?

   A. Equal Credit Opportunity Act
   B. Fair and Accurate Credit Transaction Act of 2003
   C. The Fair Credit Reporting Act
   D. Truth in Lending Act

72. What does the phrase "For Sale by Owner" mean?

   A. A sale is being facilitated by an agent
   B. Investors are open to receiving offers
   C. A property sale is being handled without a real estate agent
   D. All of the above

73. What is the name of the document used to summarize all the fees incurred by the lender and borrower during settlement of a loan?

    A. Financial statement
    B. Invoice
    C. IOU
    D. Settlement statement

74. Which entity determines the assessed value of a property?

    A. Building Inspector
    B. Municipal council
    C. Real estate agent
    D. Tax assessor

75. If a property is taxed at 40% with a tax levy of $88,000, what is its assessed value?

    A. $220,000
    B. $146,666
    C. $123,200
    D. None of the above

76. Which type of estate has rights to the property for an indefinite duration?

    A. List estate
    B. Estate for years
    C. Freehold estate
    D. Less-than-freehold estate

77. Which of the following is **not** an essential element of a deed?

    A. Signature of the grantee
    B. Date
    C. Identification of the grantor and grantee
    D. Adequate description of the property

78. What is a lessor?

    A. A person who leases real estate property from the owner of said property
    B. A person that makes a grant
    C. The owner of real estate who leases the property to another
    D. The person who transfers property by sale

79. What is the definition of a joint tenancy?

    A. When property is held by two or more parties
    B. When a third-party trust owns the property
    C. When the seller and the buyer both own the property
    D. When the property is inherited by a family member

80. What is the definition of a trust deed?

    A. The owner of the real estate property who leases the property to another
    B. A deed with limited or no warranties
    C. A deed that transfers property to a family member
    D. A document used when one party has taken out a loan from another party to purchase property

81. _____ refers to land and buildings that need to be held for a long period of time to pay for themselves.

   A. Fixity
   B. Nonhomogeneity
   C. Situs
   D. Datum

82. A shop owner leases a space in a strip mall for 2 years. The strip mall is sold to a new owner during the duration of the lease. What is the status of the lease?

   A. The lease is void
   B. The new property owner and tenant must honor all the terms of the original lease
   C. The new property owner has the right to make changes to the lease within 30 days of the sale
   D. The lease starts fresh with the new property owner as the landlord

83. A homeowner's association does not allow owners to have pets. This is an example of a _____ clause.

   A. Possessions
   B. Contingency
   C. Restricted covenants
   D. Defeasance

84. Tenancy by the entirety is only applicable to _____.

   A. Homeowners with an FHA loan
   B. Low income homeowners
   C. Recently divorced couples
   D. Married couples

85. A building inspector must provide a(an) _____ before the property can be used.

    A.   Certificate of occupancy
    B.   Quitclaim deed
    C.   Pre-qualification
    D.   Examination of title

86. Which of the following is a type of zoning?

    A.   Rural
    B.   Business
    C.   Vacation
    D.   Landmark

87. A _____ is a real estate professional that performs a visual survey of a property's structure.

    A.   Developer
    B.   Broker
    C.   Real estate appraiser
    D.   Home inspector

88. Which of the following is an example of a special purpose real property?

    A.   Farm
    B.   Public school
    C.   Timeshare
    D.   Condominium

89. _____ is the 2nd largest purchaser of the secondary market and buys mainly FHA and VA loans.

A. Federal National Mortgage Association
B. U.S. Housing and Urban Development
C. Government National Mortgage Association
D. Federal Housing Administration loan

90. Which of the following is not an economic characteristic of land?

A. Scarcity
B. Permanence of investment
C. Size
D. Improvements

91. A _____ is a provision in a mortgage that can make the debt immediately due if the borrower sells the property.

A. Acceleration clause
B. Alienation clause
C. Prepayment clause
D. Defeasance clause

92. Which survey system was adopted in 1785, and is also called the Public Land Survey System or Rectangular Survey System?

A. Geographic Information System
B. Tallahassee Meridian
C. Government Survey System
D. Principal Meridian

93. What is condemnation?

    A. The right the government has to acquire privately owned property for public use
    B. Occurs when the government seizes private property and compensates the owner
    C. Occurs when the government seizes private property and does not compensate the owner
    D. The right the government has to take privately owned property for private use

94. Which organization purchases conventional loans from savings and loans to promote stability and affordability in the housing market?

    A. Federal Home Loan Mortgage Corporation
    B. U.S. Housing and Urban Development
    C. Federal Housing Administration
    D. National Realtors Association

95. Which factors affect the demand of real estate?

    A. Population
    B. Employment
    C. Demographics
    D. All of the above

96. Which rights give the owner the right to access water when property is adjacent to a lake or an ocean?

    A. Littoral rights
    B. Riparian rights
    C. Quitclaim deed
    D. Easement

97. A _____ is a process that releases the borrower from the obligation of debt once all mortgage payment terms are met.

    A. Acceleration clause
    B. Defeasance clause
    C. Alienation clause
    D. None of the above

98. Also called restrictive covenants, this limits how a piece of real estate can be used.

    A. Reconveyance
    B. Zoning ordinances
    C. Deed restrictions
    D. Arbitration

99. Which legal document establishes one debt as inferior to another debt for collecting repayment from a debtor?

    A. Purchase agreement
    B. Closing disclosure
    C. Property deed
    D. Subordination agreement

100. Which law requires financial institutions to maintain, report and disclose loan information regarding mortgages?

    A. Home Mortgage Disclosure Act
    B. Community Reinvestment Act
    C. Real Estate Settlement Procedures Act
    D. Truth in Lending Act

THIS IS THE END OF THE NATIONAL PORTION.

State Portion

1. Which International building code did Georgia adopt?

   A. International Building Code 2018
   B. International Residential Building Code 2018
   C. International Fire Code 2018
   D. All of the above were adopted

2. Which law requires subdivisions of 100+ unimproved lots or condos to be registered with HUD?

   A. Georgia Interstate Land Sales Full Disclosure Act
   B. Interstate Land Sales Full Disclosure Act
   C. Federal Full Disclosure Act
   D. Georgia Full Disclosure Act

3. When a salesperson faxes listing to potential buyers which of the following information is required?

   A. Name of the listing firm
   B. Phone number of the listing firm
   C. Seller information
   D. A&B only

4. Which of the following is not a part of the ad valorem tax process?

   A. Budget
   B. Property Appraisal
   C. Appropriation
   D. Levy

5. Which of the following is not a part of the ad valorem tax process?

   A. Verbal consent
   B. Written authorization
   C. A retainer to the licensee
   D. All of the above will establish fiduciary duty

6. In Georgia, a realtor is required disclose a _____ to a buyer of property.

   A. Material fact
   B. Homicide
   C. Death occurred in the home
   D. All of the above is required

7. Which of the following is an example of material facts?

   A. Leaky roof
   B. Previous tenant information
   C. Property lien
   D. A&C only

8. Which type of listing allows for numerous licensees to list the property but allows only the licensee who sells the property to receive commission?

   A. Express listing
   B. Open listing
   C. Net listing
   D. Non-exclusive agency listing

9. Georgia Stigmatized Property Law states that some disclosures are not required unless _____.

   A. The seller is directly involved
   B. The buyer will be adversely affected
   C. The buyer specifically asks for the information
   D. None of the above

10. Which of the following is not a fiduciary duty?

    A. Honesty
    B. Agency Disclosure
    C. Material Facts Disclosure
    D. Misrepresentation

11. What is a principal?

    A. The interest accrued on commission
    B. A person who authorizes another person to act on their behalf
    C. The total profit to a seller who is selling property
    D. None of the above

12. What is the first offense penalty for violating the Federal Fair Housing law?

    A. $55,000
    B. $100,000
    C. $50,000
    D. $110,000

13. Which act sets rules for commercial emails and gives the recipient the right to unsubscribe from commercial emails?

    A.   Georgia SPAM Act
    B.   Commercial Messaging Act
    C.   SPAM Act
    D.   CAN-SPAM Act

14. _____ is the act of inducing owners to sell by making them believe minority individuals are moving into the area or neighborhood.

    A.   Redlining
    B.   Arbitration
    C.   Blockbusting
    D.   Basis

15. Which of the following is an exception to the Interstate Land Sales Full Disclosure Act?

    A.   Subdivisions with lots 20 acres or more
    B.   Subdivisions with fewer than 15 lots
    C.   Subdivisions with 10-25 lots
    D.   Subdivisions with lots 25 acres or more

16. An exclusive contract that has a definite termination date can be terminated by which of the following actions?

    A.   Expiration of contract only
    B.   Sale of the property
    C.   Mutual agreement between licensee and principal
    D.   All of the above

17. Who provides the earnest money during a sale?

    A. The broker
    B. The seller
    C. The buyer
    D. The lender

18. Which type of broker has little to no interaction with a real broker and charges lower commission than a real broker?

    A. Listing broker
    B. Salesperson
    C. An attorney
    D. Discount broker

19. In Georgia, which instrument is used to secure a debt on property?

    A. Securing debt deed
    B. Deed to secure debt
    C. Deed of security
    D. Deed of debt

20. Which type of loan is protected against loss if the owner fails to repay the loan?

    A. Federal loans
    B. VA-guaranteed loans
    C. Loans with a 30% or more down payment
    D. There is no such loan

21. Which Georgia law governs the agency relationships of brokers with sellers, buyers, landlords, and tenants?

    A. The Brokerage Relationships in Real Estate Transactions Act
    B. The Brokerage Relationships Act
    C. The Real Estate Transactions Act
    D. The Brokerage Act

22. If an agency contract does not have a termination date, then when will it terminate?

    A. When the home is sold
    B. When the principal decides to terminate
    C. In one year
    D. It cannot be terminated

23. In a dual agency, the broker is required to _____.

    A. Disclose to both parties of the dual agency
    B. Maintain fiduciary responsibilities to both parties
    C. Remain neutral
    D. All of the above

24. Which type of contract is derived from actions?

    A. Void contract
    B. Express contract
    C. Implied contract
    D. Executory contract

25. When material facts are misrepresented with no intent to deceive the other party it is called _____.

    A. Negative fraud
    B. Constructive fraud
    C. Negative fraud
    D. Mutual mistake

26. What are the broker's duties upon termination of an agency termination?

    A. To keep information confidential as requested
    B. To pay back any funds given by the principal
    C. To account for undistributed property or funds
    D. A&C only

27. This type of loan is a line of credit that is given to a loan originator and the funds are used to pay for a mortgage the borrower has used to purchase property?

    A. Warehousing loan
    B. Microloan
    C. Mortgage loan originator
    D. Mortgage credit

28. Which document(s) is required by the RESPA during closing?

    A. Federal Closing Document
    B. Uniform Settlement Statement
    C. Settlement Statements
    D. All are required

29. This federal law requires a lender to disclose the exact cost of credit on loans.

    A. Truth-in-Lending Law
    B. Lending Transparency Law
    C. Lending Law
    D. There is no such law

30. How can an open listing be terminated?

    A. Rescinding of sale by owner
    B. Abandonment by the broker
    C. Owner moves to another state
    D. All of the above

31. Which of the following is not an essential element of a contract?

    A. Competent parties
    B. Notoriety
    C. Mutual assent
    D. All of the above are essential elements

32. Undue influence is _____.

    A. When the principal signs a contract with a referred licensee
    B. Not voidable
    C. Voidable by the harmed party
    D. When a family member suggests selling a home for a lower price

33. This rule states that a written contract takes precedence over an oral one.

    A. Evidence rule
    B. Parole Evidence Rule
    C. The Law of Contracts
    D. There is no such rule

34. What is supervening illegality?

    A. When a regulation makes the object of an offer illegal
    B. When a court order is passed to legally allowing something that would be illegal
    C. When a brokerage takes a different path to avoid illegal actions
    D. Both B&C

35. A _____ is when an old obligation is substituted with a new obligation.

    A. Redlining
    B. Arbitration
    C. Novation
    D. Blockbusting

36. Which type of contract is unilateral and the owner agrees to sell or lease property within a certain period of time or a certain price?

    A. Option contracts
    B. Bilateral contract
    C. Lease to buy
    D. Non-exclusive contracts

37. Which statement is true about leases longer than 1 year?

    A. A tenant must provide 60-day notice before moving out
    B. If not renewed, the tenant is required to move out and it cannot be rented month to month
    C. Are illegal
    D. Must be written to be enforceable

38. Which of the following is a requirement for a valid lease?

    A. Legally competent parties
    B. Genuine assent
    C. Mutual agreement
    D. All of the above are requirements for a valid lease

39. Which of the following is not a covenant granted to a tenant?

    A. Quiet enjoyment
    B. To change the property as needed
    C. Contract rent
    D. Market rent

40. What is a maximum amount a Georgia landlord can charge as security deposit?

    A. 1 month's rent
    B. $5,000
    C. 2x the monthly rent
    D. There is no limit

41. A landlord pays _____ unless specified in the contract.

    A. Ad valorem tax
    B. Cleaning fees
    C. Renter's insurance
    D. All of the above

42. Which of the following is true about leasing property?

    A. A tenant can refuse to accept the property if possession is not given at an agreed upon time
    B. A landlord can enter the premises without permission
    C. A landlord can evict the tenant at any time for any reason
    D. All of the above are true

43. A _____ is when the seller holds legal title of property until the contract is satisfied.

    A. Assignment of contract
    B. Land sale contract
    C. Option contract
    D. Bilateral contract

44. A _____ is a clause in an agreement that the tenant and landlord agree to a periodic adjustment of monthly payments.

    A. Net lease
    B. Graduated lease
    C. Landlord inflation protection clause
    D. Inflation clause

45. Which of the following actions can a landlord take if a tenant default?

    A.   Seizure of personal property
    B.   Unlawful detainer
    C.   Eviction
    D.   All of the above

46. A _____ works with contracts, association employees, board members, and owners. They also act as a buffer between directors and owners.

    A.   Property manager
    B.   Community association manager
    C.   Salesperson
    D.   Broker

47. Which of the following is a reason for lease termination?

    A.   Expiration
    B.   Notice
    C.   Mutual agreement
    D.   All of the above

48. Which of the following is not a duty of a property manager?

    A.   Sell units
    B.   Marketing
    C.   Collecting rent
    D.   Keeping tenants

49. A _____ is a contract servicing as evidence of debt.

    A. Promissory note
    B. Title theory
    C. Borrower's statement
    D. Lender's note

50. A(n) _____ is difficult to calculate and is the actual value of the property over a period of time?

    A. Curable depreciation
    B. Incurable deprecation
    C. Physical deterioration
    D. Accrued depreciation

51. Which type of obsolescence arises from forces outside the property?

    A. Functional obsolescence
    B. Technological obsolescence
    C. Economic obsolescence
    D. Legal obsolescence

52. Which type of commercial lease has the landlord paying all property charges and the tenant paying a flat amount?

    A. Gross lease
    B. Net lease
    C. Capital lease
    D. Modified gross lease

THIS IS THE END OF THE STATE PORTION.

Answer Key – National Portion

1.	D	21.	B	41.	D	61.	B	81.	A
2.	D	22.	A	42.	C	62.	D	82.	B
3.	B	23.	B	43.	B	63.	A	83.	C
4.	A	24.	A	44.	B	64.	B	84.	D
5.	D	25.	B	45.	B	65.	A	85.	A
6.	A	26.	D	46.	A	66.	B	86.	A
7.	D	27.	A	47.	B	67.	B	87.	D
8.	D	28.	A	48.	A	68.	A	88.	B
9.	B	29.	C	49.	A	69.	B	89.	C
10.	B	30.	C	50.	C	70.	C	90.	C
11.	A	31.	C	51.	C	71.	A	91.	B
12.	D	32.	D	52.	D	72.	C	92.	C
13.	B	33.	B	53.	A	73.	D	93.	B
14.	A	34.	B	54.	B	74.	D	94.	A
15.	B	35.	D	55.	B	75.	A	95.	D
16.	B	36.	B	56.	A	76.	C	96.	A
17.	C	37.	A	57.	D	77.	A	97.	B
18.	C	38.	C	58.	A	78.	C	98.	C
19.	D	39.	A	59.	C	79.	A	99.	D
20.	D	40.	D	60.	B	80.	D	100.	A

1.   **D) All of the above**

Commercial property includes mixed use buildings (e.g. retail store on the first floor, residences above) office buildings, hotels, retail stores, multifamily houses, industrial warehouses, and more.

2.   **D) Steering**

Steering is the act of guiding prospective buyers to specified settlement areas based on race, religion and other discriminatory factors.

3.   **B) Net lease**

This is a lease where the tenant pays rent and part of utilities fee and property taxes. The landlord is tasked with paying the utility bills and property taxes that are not covered by the tenant. This lease is common in commercial real estate.

4.   **A) Lis Pendens**

This is a legal notice that a lawsuit concerning a real estate property is pending. Usually involves a property title or claims of ownership interest. Details of a property whose title is in question are required to be filed at the county record to notify future buyers and lenders.

5.   **D) Zoning Board of Appeals**

The Zoning Board of Appeals is a board of select members that is given jurisdiction to hear and decide on appeals regarding zoning laws.

6.   **A) Mortgage Banker**

A mortgage banker is an individual who originates, closes and funds with his own funds or that of a company. Once a mortgage is originated it is either retained or sold to an investor. A mortgage banker has the power to approve or reject a mortgage and earns fees on the origination of a loan.

7.   **D) Sheathing**

Sheathing is a covering structure and acts as a case for the exterior of the home. Usually used to describe a boarding material that forms the roof, floor and walls. It provides a surface for other materials and strengthens weather resistance.

8.   **D) Landlord**

A security deposit is an amount equaling monthly rent that is paid to ensure rent will be paid and to cater for other responsibilities highlighted in the lease. Can also be used as security for unpaid rent and damages and is held onto by the landlord.

9.   **B) Effective age**

This is an estimate of a building age based on its utilities and the wear and tear. It could be the actual age or a little more or less than the actual age. This is dependent on maintenance, remodeling and removal of inadequacies. It is used to determine the remaining life of a building.

10.   **B) Three years**

Brokers are required by law to hold on to a copy of property files for a minimum of 3 years. This is to act as a proof in case of a dispute in the future. These include copies of all listings, deposit receipts, cancelled checks and trust records executed or obtained during the transaction.

11. **A) British Thermal Unit**

Defined as the amount of heat required to raise the temperature of one pound of water by one-degree Fahrenheit. In the case of air conditioning, it is defined as the number of BTU per hour products that can be added or removed from the air.

12. **D) Habendum clause**

This is a legal agreement that involves the rights and interests of a property being transferred to a lessee. For a leased property there is a transfer of ownership and restrictions on the property. A purchased property is void of restrictions and only transfers ownership.

13. **B) Passive**

This is an income source that requires little to no daily input in order to yield returns.

14. **A) Ground lease**

This is a lease agreement where a tenant is allowed to develop a parcel of land during the lease period. On expiry of the lease, all improvements remain in the owner's custody. Land leases are often last between 50-99 with other agreement allowing for renewal.

15. **B) Building codes**

These are a set of regulations that are put in place to ensure design, construction, alteration and maintenance of structures is done according to the state's requirements. They aim at safeguarding the health, safety and welfare of the occupants.

16. **B) $335,051**

$325,000 / (1 - 0.03) = $335,051

17. **C) A fixture**

A fixture is any physical property that is permanently attached to real property (usually land). Fixtures are treated as a part of real property. Examples of fixtures are ceiling fans and TV mounts.

18. **C) Offsite improvements**

Offsite improvements are amenities that are not within the premise of the structure but are necessary to maximize the use of the property and ultimately increase the value of the property.

19.   **D) Joint tenancy**

Joint tenancy is a form of ownership in which several people own a property together, each with equal shares and rights. If one of the owners in a joint tenancy dies, that owner's share in the property is automatically passed to the remaining owners.

20.   **D) Preventive maintenance**

In order to maintain tenants and an acceptable return on an investment, routine checks and repairs have to be done. These are done to safeguard against failing which may incur losses to the property manager that arise due to cost of replacement.

21.   **B) CERCLA**

The Comprehensive Environmental Response Compensation and Liability Act of 1980 was enacted in order to identify, investigate and facilitate cleanup of hazardous sites. The act is currently administered by the Environmental Protection Agency.

22.   **A) A shared tenancy in which each holder has a distinct, separately transferable interest**

This type of ownership is characterized by ownership between two or more people who can have either equal or unequal shares. Unlike a joint tenancy, if an owner dies, the person's share is passed to his/her heirs and not distributed to the remaining owners.

23.   **B) Cash flow**

This is the amount of profit retained after paying off all operating costs and repurposing amounts made in dividends for use in future repairs. To be able to profit from an investment, one must maintain a positive cash flow.

24.   **A) A lien that arises without the property owner's consent**

Involuntary liens are placed by government facilities for unpaid taxes.

25.   **B) Homestead property**

Homestead laws are laws that exist to ensure to protect owners from losing their home equity while filing for bankruptcy. Homestead property enables an individual to declare a portion of property as homestead to avoid forced sale.

26.   **D) Special agent**

This is an agent engaged to perform a specific duty for a client. Their authority is limited to that particular task that translates in the expiry of the contract once the task is completed.

27.   **A) Bundle of rights**

These are legal rights that are granted to a property buyer which include right to possession, control, exclusion, enjoyment and disposition. A property owner is automatically granted the bundle of rights. In a commercial property, different rights can be assigned to different parties.

28.   **A) $1,000**

Violation of license laws may result in suspension of a license or a fine of not more than $1,000 paid to the Department of State. A reprimand is given together with the fine.

29.   **C) 39 years**

After 39 years a commercial property is eligible for applying for value loss by depreciation in order to reduce property taxes levied

30.   **C) Proration**

Proration occurs during corporate action to ensure all shareholders are treated fairly and a company does not deviate from its original target. Shareholders are offered equity or cash and required to elect one. Once the election is done, shareholders are compensated and if the shares or cash are not enough to satisfy the election each shareholder gets their due in both equity and cash.

31.   **C) 7.48 gallons**

32.   **D) Operating statement**

An operating statement is a financial statement that is done monthly and annually to document the expenses incurred and revenue gained. From the statement one can calculate the net profit or loss within the period.

33.   **B) Condop**

This is a real estate building where the housing units are divided into co-op residential units and condos. They offer more flexible rules than a co-op. Condo units are retained or sold separately by the developer.

34.   **B) General Agent**

This is an agent that is mandated to represent the principal in more than one affair.

35. **D) Usury**

These are laws that are laws set in place to protect borrowers from abusive lending such as imposing unusually high interest rates. Lenders usually target with little knowledge on the traditional loan system. An APR is usually set to protect buyers from being exploited by lenders.

36. **B) Leasehold**

This is a title on a property being leased and scheduled payments are made throughout the term of the lease. Improvements made within the property are either expensed or capitalized depending on their values.

37. **A) Mortgage**

A mortgage is a voluntary lien taken out to raise funds to buy a property. The lien is entered willingly and therefore possession of the property remains with the debtor.

38. **C) Tenancy in sufferance**

In this case, a tenant is granted the privilege to live within the premise before landlord decides to ask the tenant to vacate. Terms of the original lease must be met during this period of time. This type of tenancy can only be terminated by a written notice given not less than 30 days before the tenant is expected to move out.

39. **A) Yes**

There are no laws restricting a real estate salesperson from working multiple jobs.

40. **D) Private investors and government agencies that buy and sell real estate mortgages**

This is where home loans and servicing rights are bought within the market. Once a home loan is obtained, it is underwritten, financed and services by a lending facility. A lending facility sells loans to the secondary mortgage market in order to replenish loaning money.

41. **D) Rights granted to a property owner on the vertical space above the property**

The air space is subject to reasonable use by neighboring buildings and aircrafts. Like with property, air rights can be leased or sold.

42. **C) Co-broking**

This is a situation where two or more agents that are involved in the same the same transaction agree to work together in order to meet the needs of both parties. In this case, the agents are legally required to act in the best interest of the clients.

43. **B) Lease assignment**

A lease assignment is a legal arrangement where the landlord allows a tenant to assign another tenant to lease the apartment. The tenant is responsible for paying rent and utility fees directly to the landlord. In the case of a lease assignment, the previous tenant is held accountable for defaults in unpaid bills by the assignee.

44. **B) $2,000**

($200,000 * 0.12) / 12 = $2,000

45. **B) Closing costs**

These are the extra costs that are usually incurred by a home buyer on top the agreed upon price. They usually include title insurance, attorney fees and lender fees. These costs are negotiable but commonly paid by buyers.

46. **A) Common charges**

These are the monthly charges that are imposed on condo and condop tenants to cover common charges and amenities. They are usually cover maintenance of shared spaces and operation expenses of a building.

47. **B) Debt to income ratio**

This is a way lenders use to calculate the ability of a borrower to manage the monthly payments required in the settlement plan. Borrowers with a higher ratio have been established to experience struggles in meeting the monthly payments. 43% has been determined to be the highest ratio that can be offered credit.

48. **A) Down payment**

A down payment is an amount paid by the buyer to the seller to secure the property. A down payment is usually paid from the buyer's savings. Contrary to common belief, there is no set percentage of down payment that should be placed on a property

49. **A) Money deposited by the buyer to the seller to show interest in the purchase of a home**

This amount is deposited to give the buyer time to look into the title, sanction an appraisal and conduct an inspection of the property. This money can be returned to the buyer only in the case of a contract breach.

50. **C) Escrow**

This arrangement involves a third party that is neutral to the transaction. Usually used to secure payment in an account that can only be released on meeting of all the terms of the agreement. An escrow account is often used in transactions that involve large amounts of money such as real estate. A listing agent open an account and once the terms are signed upon by both the buyer and the seller, the deal is closed.

51. **C) Notice of termination**

This is a notice given to a tenant to end tenancy stating the reason for termination of tenancy, the date by which the tenant is required to vacate the premise and the legal implication of refusing to move.

52. **D) Notice to quit**

This is a notice given by the landlord regarding someone living in the home as a squatter. The notice usually states that the tenant is required to vacate the property within 10 days and the implications of failing to do so.

53. **A) Notice of cessation**

This is notice given by the contractor by the contractee to state that no work regarding construction has been done for a specified period of time. This notice is given in order to begin mechanical liens compensation.

54. **B) Home inspection**

They are an important part of the real estate transaction as one is able to identify the condition of the property being bought. Inspection of facilities such as plumbing, fixtures and foundation condition comes in handy in determining the value of the property.

55. **B) Convertible ARM**

This is a mortgage plan that allows an individual to benefit from the falling interest rates with the option of switching to a fixed-rate payment plan at a small fee. This switch can be made within the second to fifth year of the mortgage payment period.

56. **A) Delinquency**

This is a situation that arises where a borrower that is legally bound with the responsibility to make necessary payments on a loan or a bond interest foregoes paying the loan. Delinquency usually results in penalties depending on the type of loan and reasons behind failed payments.

57.   **D) Federal Housing Administration**

This is United States Agency whose goal is to enable low income individual acquire mortgage loans. The agency approves and insures the lenders. An FHA loan requires a loan down payment and a credit score of at least 580.

58.   **A) Consumer Financial Protection Bureau**

This is a regulatory agency that is tasked with the responsibility of overseeing the products and services offered to consumers by financial institutions. In the event of mishandling of a consumer, a complaint is filed to the CFPB for resolution.

59.   **C) Multiple Listing Service**

This is a system employed by real estate broker that allows them to view each other's listings. Sharing the database amongst a group of brokers enables brokers to identify buyers for properties they are engaged in.

60.   **B) Home warranty**

This is a contract made to ensure the cost of maintaining a household are met. It is put in place as a legal assurance that the property is fit for its intended purpose and meets the expectations of the buyer. It is usually taken to protect against expensive home repairs.

61.   **B) Escalation clause**

This is a contract that allows a buyer to set a selling price but any offers higher than the stated price will automatically lead to an increase in the set price. This gives sellers an option to outbid each other and help in making the decision for the sale price.

62.   **D) Notice of intent**

This is a non-binding proposal between a buyer and seller of a property to negotiate terms of a real estate transaction. It is usually detailed and lays key points on the weight of the transaction. It is usually used to determine the seriousness of the prospective buyer on the property.

63.   **A) Appreciation**

This is the increase in the value of an asset over a period of time. It usually occurs due to increased demand or weakening supply.

64.   **B) Biweekly mortgage**

This is a mortgage that requires a principal and interest payment plan every two weeks. It usually has a reduced interest rate throughout the lifespan of the loan.

65.   **A) Addendum**

This is an attached document that is usually included as part of the contract during the preparation. It can act as an informal explanatory attachment or to indicate other requirements of the contract that have not been included in the main attachment.

66.   **B) Cash out refinance**

This is where a homeowner refinances a mortgage for more than its value and withdraws the difference amount as cash. It is only possible to borrowers with a 20% equity on their mortgage.

67.   **B) Department of Buildings**

In order to ensure that building codes are adhered to and construction and renovations are done by professionals, a building permit is required for any building or renovation project. A building permit is a go ahead issued by local government to a contractor to construct or remodel a building. It is issued to ensure that building codes are adhered to and standards are maintained.

68.   **A) Closing**

This is the final stage of a real estate transaction. At this point, the date where contract becomes active is agreed on. On the closing date, the property is legally transferred from the seller to the buyer.

69.   **B) Commission**

This is the percentage earned by a real estate agent for effort placed in facilitating the transaction. It is usually between 5-6% of the sales price and is paid by the seller on closing. It is usually split between the buyer's and seller's agent.

70.   **C) Discount points**

Also referred to as mortgage points, these are fees paid directly to a lender by a homebuyer at closing time. They are usually paid in exchange for lower interest rates reducing monthly payments on the mortgage.

71.   **A) Equal Credit Opportunity Act**

This act was enacted in 1974 and rules it unlawful for lenders to discriminate against loan applicants based on gender, race, age and religion.

72. **C) A property sale is being handled without a real estate agent**

This phrase is used to declare that a property sale is being handled without a real estate agent. While using real estate agents to facilitate sale, some home sellers would rather avoid agents in order to save on the amount spent on commission. In this case the seller must disclose that they are not using an agent.

73. **D) Settlement statement**

This is a document that is usually used to summarize expenses incurred during a loan translation and varies according to loan types. It is usually part of the closing package that must be reviewed and signed by the borrower when closing a loan. A comprehensive settlement statement is legally required for every loan.

74. **D) Tax assessor**

An official whose responsibility is to determine the value of each taxable property in a region.

75. **A) $220,000**

$88,000 / 0.4 = $220,000

76. **C) Freehold estate**

An estate that has exclusive rights of the property for an undefined length of time. The three types of freehold estates are fee simple absolute, fee simple defeasible and life estate.

77. **A) Signature of the grantee**

The grantee does not need to sign a deed. A deed needs to be in writing, must be signed by the grantor, the grantor must have the legal capacity to transfer the property, the grantor and grantee must be identified, the property must be described adequately, the deed must be legally delivered to the grantee and the grantee must accept the deed.

78. **C) The owner of real estate who leases the property to another**

A person who grants a lease to someone else. This person is the owner of the real estate and leases it a lessee through an agreement.

79. **A) When property is held by two or more parties**

It is an agreement in which two or more people own a property with equal rights and obligations. Joint tenancy is typically entered at the same time and through a deed. If one of the owners were to die their portion of the property would automatically pass to the survivors.

80. **D) A document used when one party has taken out a loan from another party to purchase property**

It represents an agreement between the borrower and the lender in which the property is held in a trust managed by a third party until the borrower pays off the loan. The legal title of the property is transferred to the third party to hold. Trust deeds are used in place of mortgages in numerous states.

81. **A) Fixity**

Also called investment permanence is property that takes a long time to pay for itself. It also refers to the fact that land cannot be moved but is in a fixed location.

82. **B) The new property owner and tenant must honor all the terms of the original lease**

Property sold with an existing lease is still valid and it must be honored by both the new owner and the tenant.

83. **C) Restrictive covenants**

Restrictive covenants are restrictions on land used to ensure the value and enjoyment of adjoining land will be preserved. This clause limits what a tenant or owner can do with property.

84. **D) Married couples**

Tenancy by the entirety is a type of concurrent estate in real property limited to married couples. Each spouse has an equal and undivided interest in the property and they mutually own the entire estate.

85. **A) Certificate of occupancy**

A building inspector must issue a certificate of occupancy after the final inspection. It is a document issued by the local government or building department that states the building is in compliance with the building codes and is suitable for occupancy.

86. **A) Rural**

There are numerous different types of zoning: rural, residential, commercial, industrial, agricultural, combination and historic.

87. **D) Home inspector**

A home inspector determines the condition of the structure. A home inspection is a non-invasive examination of the home condition and should not be confused with an appraisal which determines the value of the property.

88.   **B) Public school**

Public schools are an example of special purpose property. It is property that is appropriate for one type of use and has a unique design. It uses special construction materials and other features which limit the use of the property.

89.   **C) Government National Mortgage Association**

The GNMA guarantees the timely payment of principal and interest on mortgage-backed securities that have been issued by approved lenders. It is also referred to as Ginnie Mae.

90.   **C) Size**

Size is not an economic characteristic of land. The economic characteristics of land are factors that affect its value in the marketplace. These are scarcity, improvements, performance of investment and location.

91.   **B) Alienation clause**

This clause states that the borrower needs to pay the mortgage in full before the borrower can transfer the property to another person. This clause will go into effect whether the property is transferred voluntarily or involuntarily.

92.   **C) Government Survey System**

This system identifies reference lines and makes up townships and sections. It has been applied to most of the land in the United States since its adoption in 1785.

93.   **B) Occurs when the government seizes private property and compensates the owner**

Condemnation occurs when the government acquires land through eminent domain. Eminent domain is the right the government has to acquire privately owned property for public use.

94.   **A) Federal Home Loan Mortgage Corporation**

This organization was created by the congress but is not a government agency and does not receive government funding. It is owned by shareholders and overseen by its board of directors.

95.   **D) All of the above**

The factors that affect demand are population, demographics, employment interest rates and borrowing costs.

96. **A) Littoral rights**

These rights are considered water rights that concern bodies of water that are static like an ocean, lake or bay. Rights for flowing water are determined by the riparian rights.

97. **B) Defeasance clause**

This clause states that a borrower will be given the title to the property once the mortgage payment terms are met. It is the final procedures in a mortgage contract.

98. **C) Deed restrictions**

Deeds restrictions are a clause in a deed that limits how real estate can be used and what can be built on the land. Most often the restrictions are not covered by community zoning regulations.

99. **D) Subordination agreement**

This agreement comes up when a home has a first and a second mortgage and the borrower would like to refinance the first mortgage. It adjusts the priority of the new loan.

100. **A) Home Mortgage Disclosure Act**

This law is used to monitor the geographic targets of mortgage lenders, provides mechanisms for predatory lending practices and provides reporting statistics on the mortgage market to the government.

Answer Key – State Portion

1.	D	21.	A	41.	A
2.	B	22.	C	42.	A
3.	D	23.	D	43.	B
4.	B	24.	C	44.	B
5.	B	25.	B	45.	D
6.	A	26.	D	46.	B
7.	D	27.	A	47.	D
8.	B	28.	B	48.	A
9.	C	29.	A	49.	A
10.	D	30.	B	50.	D
11.	B	31.	B	51.	C
12.	A	32.	C	52.	A
13.	D	33.	B		
14.	C	34.	A		
15.	A	35.	C		
16.	D	36.	A		
17.	C	37.	D		
18.	D	38.	D		
19.	B	39.	B		
20.	B	40.	D		

1. **D) All of the above were adopted**

    All of the following were adopted. Other codes adopted were the International Plumbing Code 2018, International Mechanical Code 2018, and International Fuel Gas Code 2018.

2. **B) Interstate Land Sales Full Disclosure Act**

    This law applies to subdivisions of 100+ unimproved lots or condo units. They also must be registered with HUD and the buyer must receive a factual report before signing an agreement. This law also gives the buyer 7 business days right of recission.

3. **D) A&B only**

    Faxes must have the name and phone number of the listing firm when faxing information to potential buyers.

4. **B) Property Appraisal**

    Property appraisal is not part of the ad valorem tax process. Assessment, equalization, and tax rate are all a part of the process.

5. **B) Written authorization**

For fiduciary duty to be established, written authorization is needed through a written contract.

6. **A) Material fact**

If a broker knows of a defect in the property, they are required to disclose it to the potential buyers. They do not, however, need to disclose death of property owners, death in the home, homicide or felony's that have occurred in the home.

7. **D) A&C only**

Material facts are considered details that may influence a buyer's decision about buyer a property or the price they pay for the property. These include information about the property in both legal and condition.

8. **B) Open listing**

This type of listing allows for numerous licensees to market the property and whoever sells the property is granted commission. If the seller sells the property, then no broker is paid commission. It is an express, unilateral, executory listing.

9. **C) The buyer specifically asks for the information**

Stigmatized property does not need to be disclosed unless it has been directly asked by the buyer. This law requires licensees to disclose heinous crimes or allegations if asked. They are not required to volunteer the information.

10. **D) Misrepresentation**

Misrepresentation is not a fiduciary duty. Honesty, agency and material fact disclosure, and account are all fiduciaries owed to the client.

11. **B) A person who authorizes another person to act on their behalf**

The principal provides another person or entity to act on their behalf. In the case of real estate, a principal is the buyer or seller who hires a real estate license to sell or buy property.

12. **A) $55,000**

The penalty for violating the Federal Fair Housing law is $55,000 for the first offense and $110,000 for the second offense.

13. **D) CAN-SPAM Act**

This act requires commercial emails to have accurate subject lines, include a postal address, ensure a clear indication that it is an act, and provide an opt-out provision. The act also has a 16,000-dollar penalty for each violating email.

14. **C) Blockbusting**

This is an illegal act by licensees or buyers to persuade owners of selling property cheaply in fear of minorities moving into that neighborhood. Then reselling the property at a higher price.

15. **A) Subdivisions with lots 20 acres or more**

Other exceptions include subdivisions with fewer than 25 lots, lots sold to builders, and subdivisions in which lots are improved.

16. **D) All of the above**

All of the above are ways a contract with a termination date can be terminated.

17. **C) The buyer**

The buyer usually provides earnest money that must be held by the licensee or a closing attorney. If the buyer backs out of the sale for specific reasons, then the seller automatically is awarded the earnest money.

18. **D) Discount broker**

This type of broker or brokerage allows clients to purchase and sell properties, but they do not provide advice, research, planning or other investment services. They typically have little or no interaction with a real broker and charge lower fees.

19. **B) Deed to secure debt**

In Georgia, in order to secure a debt on property the instrument is called a deed to secure debt or security debt. The lender is deeded the property in a lesser form of a deed that becomes activated if the borrower defaults in some way.

20. **B) VA-guaranteed loan**

This type of loan is made by a private lender and the guaranty states that the lender is protected against loss if the owner fails to repay the loan.

21. **A) The Brokerage Relationships in Real Estate Transactions Act**

Also called BRETTA, this is a law that's intent is to not interfere with the contractual relationships agreed upon by the parties involved.

22. **C) In one year**

If the agency agreement has not specified a date of termination, then the termination date is automatically one year from the agreement being signed.

23. **D) All of the above**

The agency in a dual agency requires all of the above, the agent must also obtain consent from both parties. They also may not reveal confidential information to anyone other than the broker.

24. **C) Implied contract**

This type of contract is created by actions and is legally binding. It derives from actions, conduct, or circumstances of one or more parties in agreement.

25. **B) Constructive fraud**

This type of fraud stems of misrepresentation with no intent to deceive or mislead the other party. It is also voidable by the injured party.

26. **D) A&C only**

BRETTA requires that the broker, after termination of duties, keep information requested by the principal confidential and to account for undistributed property or funds.

27. **A) Warehousing loan**

This is a loan that is used to pay for a mortgage when purchasing property. The life of this loan extends from its origination to the time it is sold on the secondary market directly or through securitization.

28. **B) Uniform Settlement Statement**

RESPA requires this real estate closing form in order to account for all funds received, disbursements made, and all expenses and credits at closing. It is also called HUD-1.

29. **A) Truth-in-Lending Law**

This law requires a lender to disclose the exact cost of credit on specific loans. This is required so the borrower can compare loans and costs from other sources before committing to a lender.

30. **B) Abandonment by the broker**

If a broker abandons an open listing than the contract can be terminated. Other ways include sale of the property and death of the owner.

31. **B) Notoriety**

Notoriety is not an essential element of a contract. Other elements include genuine assent and valuable consideration.

32. **C) Voidable by the harmed party**

This occurs when someone is influenced to sign a contract by another because of a relationship of trust and confidence.

33. **B) Parole Evidence Rule**

This rule says that written contracts take precedence over oral ones. It prevents a party in a written contract from presenting extrinsic evidence.

34. **A) When a regulation makes the object of an offer illegal**

This change in law makes the obligations under a contract legally impossible.

35. **C) Novation**

This is replacing someone or something in a contract with someone or something else. All parties must agree, and this replaces the original contract with a new one.

36. **A) Option contracts**

In this type of contract, a buyer leases a property with the option to buy it.

37. **D) Must be written to be enforceable**

Any lease that is for over 1 year, needs to be in written or else it is not enforceable.

38. **D) All of the above are requirements for a valid lease**

The listed are requirements. Other requirements consideration, legal purpose, in writing, description of the premises, lease term, signature, delivery and acceptance.

39.   **B) To change the property as needed**

The tenant is not free to change rented property as need. Other uses of the premises include restrictive covenant and protective covenant.

40.   **D) There is no limit**

There is no limit in Georgia regarding the amount a landlord may charge as a security deposit. However, it must be returned within 30 days from the end of the lease.

41.   **A) Ad valorem tax**

The landlord is responsible for paying ad valorem tax as well as insurance unless specified otherwise.

42.   **A) A tenant can refuse to accept the property if possession is not given at an agreed upon time**

If the landlord does not give possession to a tenant at the agreed upon time, the tenant can refuse to accept the property. The landlord also, cannot enter the property, after possession, without permission.

43.   **B) Land sale contract**

This type of contract is a form of seller financing. Similar to a mortgage but the buyer makes payments to the owner instead of borrowing money from a lender or bank.

44.   **B) Graduated lease**

This is an escalator clause that protects from rising costs and inflation.

45.   **D) All of the above**

All of the listed are actions a landlord can take. They can also sue for rental payment or damages and accelerate due date of remaining rent payments.

46.   **B) Community association manager**

This manager also is a buffer between directors and owners. A community association maintains and operates rec facilities, enforces protective covenants, and collects dues and assessments.

47.   **D) All of the above**

All of the above are reasons a lease can be terminated. A merger, condemnation, eviction, destruction of the premises and death are other reasons.

48.   **A) Sell units**

Selling units is not a duty of a property agent. Other duties include property maintenance and accounting and reporting.

49.   **A) Promissory note**

This document is evidence of debt. It is the borrower's obligation to pay back the mortgage and a promise to pay back the loan.

50.   **D) Accrued depreciation**

This type of depreciation is reduction of actual value over a period of time. Some of the main reasons is wear and tear and obsolescence.

51.   **C) Economic obsolescence**

This type of obsolescence is depreciation that is caused by factors not on the property, in the property, or within the property lines. Examples of this include a neighborhood experiencing a rise in crime or problems in the job market.

52.   **A) Gross lease**

In this type of lease, the landlord pays for all charges that occur such as insurance premiums, repairs, and maintenance.

Resources

3.1 Finding a broker

Now that you've passed the exam, it's time to officially become an agent! Below is a list of companies and their websites to help you expedite your job search and help you start your journey in selling your first property!

BHHS Georgia Properties – https://www.bhhsgeorgia.com/
Broadmoor Realty Company – https://www.homesincolumbusga.com/
Chapman Hall Realtors – https://www.chapmanhallrealtorsatlantanorth.com/
Coldwell Banker SSK – https://www.coldwellbankerssk.com/milledgeville-georgia-real-estate/
Curry Companies – http://www.currycompanies.com/
Fickling & Company Realtors – https://www.fickling.com/homes-for-sale-macon-georgia.html
GTL Real Estate – https://www.centralgeorgiarealty.com/
Harmon & Harmon Realtors, Inc. – http://harmonandharmon.com/
Harry Norman – https://www.harrynorman.com/offices/1313-Peachtree-City
Keg Realtors – https://kegrealtors.com/
Keller Williams Realty – https://kwmiddlega.yourkwoffice.com/
Pinnacle Search Partners, LLC – https://www.pinnaclesearch.com/
Plantation Creek Real Estate Company, LLC – https://www.plantationcreekrealestate.com/
Rivoli Realtors – https://www.rivolirealty.com/
Savannah Real Estate Company – https://savannahrealestate.com/

Sheridan Solomon & Associates – https://sheridansolomon.com/
Statesboro Real Estate – https://www.buystatesboro.com/
The Real Estate Company – http://www.therealestatecompany.biz/
Tom Peterson Realtors – https://www.tompetersonrealtors.com/
North Realty Georgia – http://www.northrealtygeorgia.com/

3.2 Interviewing

Congratulations! You did get the interview. Now, just a little work and you can ace it!

First, start by going to all of the social media pages associated with your potential employer. Focus on several interesting things that they do and specialize in. Look at which type of listings they are showing on their pages and what types of neighborhoods they appear for listings. Look up the particular broker you are interviewing with and go to his/her LinkedIn page and learn more about her/him.

While you're looking at your potential employer's social media pages, take a look at your own. Are there any posts on your Facebook or other social media sites that need to be removed? Employers are looking at your pages. Anything inappropriate needs to go!

Real estate is all about creating a network of potential clients who trust that what you're selling to them will meet their needs. This means you must understand to differentiate between a client looking to buy a house to raise their newborn and a client who is looking for long term appreciation.

Try simulating cold calls by opening up random properties on Zillow or Trulia, studying them for 2 minutes, and then trying to sell your friend on these properties. They will most likely be asking similar questions to actual prospective buyers or sellers, so it's a very useful exercise in preparing yourself for the mock cold call during the interview.

In addition, study the geography of your broker's city to make sure you don't go in completely blind. Get familiar with the prices and trends in those areas and even take a tour. Drive or walk around and know the neighborhood like the back of your hand so you can impress the employer

On the day of the interview choose your outfit carefully. You should wear some type of suit and make sure your shoes are in good condition. Ask a friend to give you input on the clothes that make you look the most professional. Make sure you brushed your teeth, and your hair is neatly styled. Make sure you don't smell of smoke as most workplaces are smoke-free. No perfume or cologne – your new office may be perfume free. Never chew gum! You will not get the job!

When you arrive at the interview, always make sure to greet the receptionist. Every person you meet at your potential future employer is important! Make a good impression.

When you land the interview, it's important to have certain answers prepared to more commonly asked questions. First, let's look at general types of questions that you may be asked at any type of interview:

1. Tell me about yourself. This is not the time to talk about everything that happened to you from birth. This is an opportunity to show off a certain drive or characteristic or hobby that is special and helps to explain why you are seeking that particular job. For example, did you participate in a lot of team sports or a lot of clubs in high school or college? Did you work on volunteer projects that required you to meet a lot of new people of all ages and work with them and/or help them? The interviewer has your resume (Always bring extras with you!), so you do not have to spout off all of your previous education and positions. Devote just a sentence or two to that part of your answer.

2. What are your greatest strengths and weaknesses? This is a very tricky question. We all know our strengths; winning personality, gets along with everyone, good at math, good at negotiating, etc., but what about our weaknesses? Well, you certainly want to be honest but now isn't the time to confess all. Choose one. Do you take too long sometimes on a project because you want every detail to be perfect? Do you sometimes want to do something completely by yourself, but you really would be better off asking others for help? These are just two examples of weaknesses that won't sound like you are unprepared for your new job.

3. Where do you see yourself in 5 years? This seems pretty straightforward but be careful. The person interviewing you could be a manager. It is best not to say that you want his/her job. Instead, it may be better to say, I see myself expanding into new roles, doing what I do better, expanding my client base, becoming more successful, continuing my real estate education, and similar phrases.

4. Why did you choose our Company? Everyone asks this question. If you haven't gone to the Company's website, don't go to the interview. You should know everything about the Company and the local office where you are interviewing. You should know which type of real estate they specialize in, how long it's been in business, any recent mergers or expansions, the physical area it is licensed to practice in, and as much as you find on their website and Facebook page and other social media.

5. Why should I hire you and not the next person? This is your moment in the spotlight. Don't just say "pick me!!". Here is a sample: "All of my life, I have enjoyed working with people; when I worked at X company or volunteered at Y organization, I was able to get along with all types of people from children to the elderly. I also have been on teams or worked on teams, and I enjoy it greatly. I like to help people, and there is no bigger purchase than a home. I believe that I have the people skills and the real estate knowledge that I need to be a successful addition to your Company.

6. Why are you leaving your current job? This is not the moment to say how much you dislike your current manager or co-worker. Always be positive at your interview. You can talk about the lack of advancement opportunities, a salary freeze, future layoff being expected, change in your current employer's office location, or some other concrete reason. You can even say that you don't feel all of your skills are being utilized, and you want to use your new knowledge every day in your job.

7. Give me an example of a situation where you used teamwork to accomplish your goal. Even if you only work by yourself at your current job, look back to previous jobs and have the answer

ready. If you don't have a job that matches, think about your volunteer activities at your children's school or at a community center or retirement village.

8. Would you rather work by yourself or as part of a team? This may be a good one to answer with a bit of vagueness. You can say that it depends on what the assignment might be. Do you have to give a major presentation to a commercial client? That might be a great time to ask for input and help as needed. Do you have to write a simple analysis of a problem? Maybe you feel more comfortable completing this on your own. You might want to say that it is very important to ask for feedback from co-workers and managers on projects and on small assignments when you have questions or reach a dead end.

9. What type of manager do you prefer? Do you prefer to work independently or to have more direction? This is always a tricky one as well. Make sure, once again, that you don't diss any of your former managers. A good response would be that you expect some direction from your manager. You feel that you know generally when you need help and would be sure to ask your manager for direction at those times. Also, you welcome all constructive feedback. It is very important to show that you are open to learning and open to change.

10. Why do you have gaps on your resume? Make sure you know the answer in advance to this question. Were you raising a family, taking care of an elderly parent, moving across the country due to a partner relocation, volunteering, etc.? Whatever it is, make sure to answer this one without any hesitation and move on.

11. What is customer service? Be careful with this one. There are two types of customers – internal and external. Everyone you work with in your office is an internal customer; others are external. The same level of consideration should be given to both internal and external customers. Speak about how important it is to answer questions, do tasks that are needed, go above and beyond the average effort, and ask for help if you don't know the answers.

12. Are you organized? No one wants to admit they are disorganized. If you are going into real estate where there are mounds of paperwork and so many different elements to keep track with, let's assume that every person interviewing for this position must be organized!

13. What do you do when several people give you tasks to do, and it is clear to you that you will not be able to finish them on time?

14. Tell me about a time when you went above and beyond what was required? Hopefully, this will be an easy one to answer. Think about a suggestion you made to your manager to take on more work when a fellow employee was out sick or a time when you thought the presentation needed a special PowerPoint and you produced it.

15. Tell me about a time you had to deal with a difficult person and how you managed to diffuse the situation? You really need to think about this one in advance. If you can't think of a difficult person in your professional life, think about a friend of a friend or someone else. Always acknowledge a difficult person's feelings and avoid arguing about strong opinions that impact an issue that isn't really that important.

16. If we offer you the position, how much notice do you have to give to your current employer? Be prepared to know the answer to this one. If you say that you can leave tomorrow, your future employer may not be pleased. It shows that you are not being loyal to your current employer by leaving them in the lurch. Two weeks is standard practice, but if you have a contract, be sure to read it.

Then, you will be asked more specific questions that are relevant to the real estate industry or this particular job. These include but are not limited to:

1. Why do you want to work in the real estate business?
2. This is a commission-based business, which means there is no ceiling to how much you can earn, but it also means there is no floor either. Are you open to this?
3. Let's go through a mock cold call together. I'll be the buyer, and you'll be the seller's agent.
4. How would you sell a property in a neighborhood you've never been to before?
5. A couple is looking to buy their first home. What kind of houses would you suggest?
6. A seasoned investor is looking for investment properties. By coincidence, the Independence Hall is for sale and you are the seller's agent. Pitch it to them.
7. A retiree is looking to sell their house. He is unsure about whether it's a good time to sell it. Explain to them why it is a good time to put the property on the market.

Be prepared to answer technical questions you may have studied for your exam such as:

1. What is the difference between a joint tenancy and a tenancy by the entireties?
2. What is the difference between a cooperative and a condominium?
3. Why is title insurance important?
4. Why would a buyer agree to lease back to a seller?
5. What are the duties of a buyer's agent?
6. What is a tax credit opposed to a tax deduction?
7. What is an easement?
8. Why would someone want to partition property, and what does this mean?
9. When would there be a lien on real estate?
10. What happens at settlement?
11. Why would a homeowner agree to finance a second mortgage for the buyer?

At the end of an interview, the interviewer will always ask if you have any questions. It is never a good idea to say, "No"! Here are some suggestions:

1. If I work here full time, what would be a range of the commissions I could expect in the first year?
2. What type of commission structure is there? Are commissions paid immediately upon closing? What types of fees am I required to pay out-of-pocket? Do I pay any advertising, computer, or other fees?
3. How often would I normally be assigned floor duty? If I answer the phone while on floor duty, do I get that listing?
4. How many open houses would I normally attend a month?
5. What is your hiring process timewise?
6. Do you pay for continuing education?

7. Although I know there isn't a truly "typical" day, what kinds of activities will I be performing during my first few weeks on the job?
8. When I attend my first settlement, will someone more senior come with me to the closing?
9. Will I attend all of the inspections for my listings?
10. What are the types of problems that arise at settlement?
11. Do you give out a list of mortgage brokers to clients?
12. How many people work in this office?
13. Is there coordination with other nearby offices – both this brand and others?
14. Do you provide a list of mortgage brokers to the buyer?

When you are finished with your interview, make sure to thank the interviewer, ask for her/his card, and thank the receptionist before you leave. Every impression counts! When you arrive home, if you really do want to work at that office, within 24 hours write a short email thank you note to your interviewer. If you don't hear back within a week, you can send a brief follow-up e-mail expressing your continuing interest in the position.

Made in the USA
Columbia, SC
21 August 2024